CAROLE LOMBARD

2 ⅛

CAROLE LOMBARD

A Pyramid Illustrated History of the Movies

by
LEONARD MALTIN

General Editor: **TED SENNETT**

PYRAMID
PUBLICATIONS
NEW YORK

*To my wonderful wife Alice for her patience
during a difficult time, and for sharing with me the
re-discovery of Carole Lombard*

CAROLE LOMBARD
A Pyramid Illustrated History of the Movies

A PYRAMID BOOK

Pyramid edition published June 1976

Library of Congress Catalog Card Number: 00-0000

Printed in the United States of America

Pyramid Books are published by Pyramid Publications (Harcourt Brace Jovanovich). Its trademarks, consisting of the word "Pyramid" and the portrayal of a pyramid, are registered in the United States Patent Office.

PYRAMID PUBLICATIONS
(Harcourt Brace Jovanovich)
757 Third Avenue, New York, N.Y. 10017

Layout and Design by ANTHONY BASILE

ACKNOWLEDGMENTS

My sincere thanks to Edward Bernds, David Chierichetti, John Cromwell, Bob Epstein of the U.C.L.A. Film Archive, William K. Everson, Lester Glassner, Herb Graff, Al Greenberg, Ron Hall, Al Kilgore, Don Koll, Don Krim of United Artists, Eddie Quillan, Charles Silver of the Museum of Modern Art, and Chris Steinbrunner for their help in the preparation of this book.

Photographs: Jerry Vermilye, The Memory Shop,
Gene Andrewski, Cinemabilia, Leonard Maltin,
and the companies that produced and distributed
the films of Carole Lombard.

CONTENTS

INTRODUCTION

Categorizing Carole Lombard as a comedienne—as most latterday writers and fans have done—is doing an injustice to one of the brightest talents that ever graced a Hollywood film.

Lombard was a superb *actress*, (as well as a great beauty) and her success in screwball-comedy roles tended to obscure the fact that she was often seen to equal advantage in dramatic films.

The image of Lombard as a "screwball" was enhanced by her off-screen shenanigans, which were legendary. An enthusiastic prankster and party-goer (as well as an imaginative party-*giver*), Carole was known to millions of fans for her unscripted antics through the pages of *Photoplay* and other fan magazines, creating an impression almost as strong as the one forged by her screen appearances.

Comedy also gave Lombard her greatest career break, after years of humdrum roles as nominal leading lady to most of Paramount's male stars. The very idea of so beautiful a woman tackling wacky comedy endeared her to thirties audiences, who then demanded that she appear in such films exclusively. When the actress bolted and sought greater variety, her popularity slipped, even though her choice of dramatic vehicles was quite sound.

Then Lombard moved into another role—as one of the reigning queens of Hollywood, the wife of movieland's undisputed "King," Clark Gable. Their seemingly perfect marital union added yet another dimension to Lombard's public image—and to her private personality.

It's nearly impossible to find a Hollywood colleague of Lombard's with a bad word to say about her. A girl who grew up in the movie world, she earned the love and respect of all who knew her, for her forthrightness, her beauty, her contagious sense of fun, and her enormous talent, although not necessarily in that order.

She swore like a sailor, looked like a million bucks, and when given the chance, outclassed and outacted all the glamour-girls and trained actresses in Hollywood.

There was only one Carole Lombard.

Carole Lombard's beginnings offered little indication of the life that was to unfold over the next thirty-three years.

The third child born to one of the "better" families in Fort Wayne, Indiana, Jane Alice Peters came into this world on October 6, 1908. Her upper-middle-class existence was shaken when her spirited mother (Elizabeth, known as Bess) took her children to California for a visit in 1914. Unbeknownst to the children, she was finding it increasingly difficult to live with their father, who had never been the same after an accident several years before. She also longed to stretch her wings in some place more exciting than Fort Wayne.

So the Peters family resettled in Los Angeles, where Jane grew up under the influence of her two older brothers, Frederic Jr. and Stuart. She was labeled a tomboy and enjoyed the company of her brothers and their male friends much more than that of girls her age.

Young Jane's interests, however, were not confined to rough-housing with the boys. She enjoyed performing, in class and neighborhood plays, and was reportedly a movie fan even before her family moved to California.

But curiously enough, her first movie role came about because a prominent director saw her in the tomboy guise. As Allan Dwan

FROM JANE TO CAROL

recalled for Peter Bogdanovich some fifty years after the fact, "I saw a kid playing baseball on the street with some other kids (It was next door to a friend of mine who was a Paramount executive). She was a cute-looking tomboy—about twelve—a hoyden, out there knocking hell out of the other kids, playing better baseball than they were. And I needed someone of her type for this picture. She'd never acted, so we talked to her parents and they let her do it and she was very good. Her name was Jane Peters and she later changed it to Carole Lombard."

The film was *A Perfect Crime*, starring Monte Blue, and Dwan's instincts were sound, since she carried off the role of Blue's younger sister quite nicely in this forgettable melodrama. But it was a one-time thing, and after filming was completed in the spring of 1921, Jane returned to school and didn't appear on-screen again for several years.

During that time, however, the young teen-ager never lost her appetite for acting, nor her desire to be a movie star. She attended a dramatic school, and among her classmates at Fairfax High were boys and girls connected in various ways with the hometown movie industry. One of them, Sally Eilers,

In the mid-twenties

A PERFECT CRIME (1921). With Monte Blue

launched her successful career about the same time as her younger classmate.

Jane's devoted mother Bessie was not a stage mother in the familiar sense of the term, but she was aware of her daughter's blossoming beauty, and encouraged her in many ways. Bess was not above touting her daughter to potential film employers, or providing an open house to those who could aid Jane's career.

In an era when a pretty face was all a girl needed to break into the movies, it was not uncommon for teen-aged students at local high schools to attract the notice of producers, agents, and talent scouts. Camerawork and makeup were such in the twenties that very young girls could be made to appear much older, especially if their roles were secondary to the male star's and didn't require extensive closeups or lengthy emotional scenes.

In 1924, Jane Peters actively sought a return to the movie world, and with her mother's help, answered several audition calls. Most of these led nowhere, but an introduction to Fox production chief Winfield Sheehan paid off with a starter's contract at fifty dollars a week. Acting talent was not the prime requisite for a stock contract at Fox or any other studio. But at sixteen, Jane (now Carol) Peters was already an exceptionally pretty girl, and Sheehan knew that she could be put to good use in Fox films.

He also felt that Carol Peters was too plain a name, and solicited ideas for a change from his new contractee. She suggested the name Lombard, recalling some family friends, and Sheehan was pleased. So Carol Lombard it was. The "e" in Carole was still six years away.

For Carol's Fox debut, she was cast in a Western starring Buck Jones. This was almost inevitable, since the leading movie cowboys were constantly in need of fresh female faces to perform obligatory love scenes in their films; over the years, many an attractive girl would get her start in Western films (among them Rita Hayworth, Jennifer Jones and Laraine Day).

Just as typically, these screen roles offered little to the budding actresses except screen billing and a salary. Some came away with sore derrieres from their first horseback rides. But at least they were working in the movies.

Carol appeared with Buck Jones three times within a matter of months. Her first role was small

HEARTS AND SPURS (1925). With Buck Jones

and unbilled, in *Gold and the Girl* (1925). In *Hearts and Spurs* (1925) she graduated to leading lady, while *Durand of the Badlands* (1925) sent her back to the second rank, behind Marion Nixon.

She was also cast—incredibly—as the leading lady in a romantic melodrama called *Marriage in Transit* (1925), directed by Roy William Neill (best known for the later Basil Rathbone *Sherlock Holmes* films) and starring up-and-coming leading man Edmund Lowe. Ludicrous as the casting of a 17-year-old girl may have seemed to insiders, she apparently came off well, with studio experts camouflaging her youth with makeup and appropriate costumes. Lowe portrayed a secret

agent who assumes the guise of a government conspirator in order to retrieve an important code. He woos and marries Celia Hathaway (Lombard), who's been linked with the *real* conspirator, but by the time the case is solved and Lowe reveals his true identity, he and Celia really do love each other and (presumably) live happily ever after.

Significant only as Lombard's first leading role, this now-lost film was apparently no great shakes. *Photoplay* called it "Secret Service Plot No. 48," but *Motion Picture News* took the trouble to say, "Edmund Lowe's leading woman, Carol Lombard, displays good poise and considerable charm."

Even so, Fox was not sufficiently interested in Lombard's "charm"

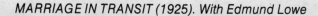

MARRIAGE IN TRANSIT (1925). With Edmund Lowe

A GOLD DIGGER OF WEEPAH (1927).
Lombard in flowered skirt. With Billy Bevan (extreme left)

to build her into a leading movie personality. She was only one of many good-looking ingenues who typified the word "starlet," kept busier shooting "cheesecake" and promotional photos than making movies. (Her role in *Dick Turpin*, a costume picture with Tom Mix, landed on the cutting-room floor.) Other, better opportunities began to present themselves, however, in 1926. There were introductions to such prestigious Fox directors as John Ford and Frank Borzage, with the promise of a role in Borzage's film *Early to Wed*. She also started shooting *The Road to Glory*, a film that marked the directorial debut of Howard Hawks.

But Carol's career was interrupted by an accident that might have spelled the end of any movie ambition.

By now, she was part of a swinging younger set that regularly attended the posh Cocoanut Grove, entering dance contests and having a good time in the midst of the roaring-twenties atmosphere in Los Angeles. Carol was returning home from a basketball game with wealthy Harry Cooper when his sporty Bugatti was involved in a crash. The force of impact shattered the windshield and lodged a piece of glass in Carol's cheek.

To anyone else, the accident would have meant a facial scar, and little else. But Carol and her mother knew that her face was her career, and quickly decided to have plastic surgery performed. The

RUN, GIRL, RUN (1928). With Jim Hallett

gash was repaired and the surgery performed in a long, painful operation during which Carol remained conscious.

Ultimately, Carol looked as good as new, with one minor flaw remaining on her cheek. She eventually became so attuned to cinematography and its tricks that she could tell cameramen the best way to camouflage this scar—and generally, they listened. But the accident curtailed her Fox contract, and led to a discouraging, dormant period.

Then, in best Hollywood fashion, the telephone rang.

It was her old schoolmate Sally Eilers, informing her that Mack Sennett was looking for a new girl to fill out his youthful "bathing beauty" roster. Sally was being promoted to stardom in Sennett's feature *The Good-bye Kiss*, although after its completion she returned to the two-reel shorts. Carol was worried about her scar, but Sennett couldn't have cared less, and signed her right away.

Lombard's tenure at the Sennett studio has been described many times, but seldom with any accuracy. Although nominally she was a "bathing beauty," this was primarily for publicity-photo purposes, and of her dozen-odd Sennett shorts, only a few had bathing beauty motifs. It is also unlikely that Lombard was involved in pie-throwing, as most accounts

THE SWIM PRINCESS (1928). With Jim Hallett, Daphne Pollard, and Barney Hellum

insist. By this time, pie-throwing was considered somewhat passé at the Sennett studio, although other slapstick indignities were still employed.

Lombard was not really a comedienne in the Sennett pictures; for the most part, she was hired on the basis of her looks, to act as girlfriend or foil for the *real* laugh-getters at the studio: mustachioed Billy Bevan, Andy Clyde, Vernon Dent, and energetic little Daphne Pollard.

Sennett's days of glory were past when Lombard joined his troupe. The one-time "King of Comedy" had been responsible for the screen careers of Charlie Chaplin, Mabel Normand, Harry Langdon, Roscoe "Fatty" Arbuckle, and dozens of other silent-movie clowns. But by the late twenties, the possibility of building new comedy stars in short-subjects was remote, and the slicker, more innovative two-reelers being turned out by his rival, Hal Roach, were leaving Sennett in second place.

The producer persisted in using the same old formulas, and before long he was considered "old-hat." But one formula that never failed was spotlighting pretty girls, and this is where Lombard fit into the Sennett scheme. Carol was young and pretty, and it didn't take her long to get into the comic spirit at Sennett's. Together with girls like Sally Eilers, Carmelita Geraghty,

THE BICYCLE FLIRT (1928). With Vernon Dent, Billy Bevan, and Dot Farley

THE GIRL FROM NOWHERE (1928). Lombard at extreme left. With Madalynne Fields and Daphne Pollard.

and Madeline Hurlock, she provided eye-appeal that nicely complemented the situation-comedy antics of her more boisterous colleagues in films like *The Girl from Everywhere* (1927), *The Beach Club* (1928), and *His Unlucky Night* (1928).

Carol was then featured in a series of campus pictures which took advantage of her athletic grace and prowess. In *Run, Girl, Run* (1928), she was cast as a sprinter, with Daphne Pollard as her excitable coach, and in *The Swim Princess* (1928), she was a swimming champ. Other collegiate comedies included *The Campus Carmen* (1928), with the dormitory

troupe putting on a mangled version of Bizet's opera, featuring all the girls in scanty costumes.

Interestingly, the Sennett films also marked Carol's debut in Technicolor, a treat denied moviegoers for a decade to come, until she made her "starring" color appearance in *Nothing Sacred*. For *Run, Girl, Run*, *The Swim Princess*, and *Campus Carmen*, Sennett shot key scenes in the early Technicolor process, hoping to boost their box-office appeal. In these, as in the black-and-white sequences, Carol photographed magnificently, her striking face easily standing out among the nameless young girls who pop-

THE CAMPUS VAMP (1928). Lombard in white hat

ulated every Sennett film.

The year Carol spent with the "King of Comedy" had several lasting benefits. First, it exposed her to comedy filmmaking and helped her to develop a light touch, as well as a sense of timing. Second, it helped to establish her name, even though in the Hollywood caste system Sennett stardom was not ranked terribly high. And third, it brought her together with Madalynne Fields, who was to become Carol's lifelong friend and advisor. At the time, "Fieldsie" was the resident fat-girl in Sennett's stock company, subject to the manifold embarrassments that the comedy troupe thought natural for

any obese woman. She and Carole were fast friends, and co-starred in several of the Sennett shorts.

At this time, Mack Sennett released his films through Pathé, which had once been a major force in American films, but was now undergoing corporate problems. Joseph P. Kennedy was in charge of the Hollywood operation, and he tried to build up his sagging studio by recruiting fresh faces, often from the ranks of Sennett players. He and Sennett had a working relationship under which contracts were interchanged.

So it was that Lombard finally returned to features. While at Sennett's, she had done a Poverty

As she appeared in POWER (1928)

Lombard in 1929

Row quickie, *The Divine Sinner* (1928), which was nothing more than a standard assignment. Now she turned to Pathé with hopes of something better; the Pathé "stars" during this period were William "Hopalong Cassidy" Boyd and Robert Armstrong, with Carol joining several newcomers whom Kennedy hoped would attract attention.

Unfortunately, the Pathé pictures seldom varied from the routine. Low budgets, as well as uninspired directors and writers, were usually at fault. Worse, Pathé was unsure about making the switch from silent films to talkies, so even promising pictures got caught in the lurch.

Lombard's Pathé feature debut was hardly auspicious. In *Power* (1928) she had a small role as one of two "dames" who capture the fancy of rough-and-tumble dam workers William Boyd and Alan Hale. The other "dame" was equally young, even less experienced Joan Bennett. Carol also landed a small part in Raoul Walsh's prestigious Fox picture, *Me, Gangster* (1928), but again, her role

SHOW FOLKS (1928). With Eddie Quillan and Bessie Barriscale

NED McCOBB'S DAUGHTER (1928). With Irene Rich

was too small for anyone to notice.

Then Pathé gave her a break, casting her in the third lead of *Show Folks* (1928), which starred another Sennett graduate, Eddie Quillan, and Lina Basquette, with Robert Armstrong in support. The film itself was nothing special, a run-of-the-mill backstage yarn, but it at least provided Carol with a genuine role, that of the "other woman" vying for Quillan's affections. No one turned handsprings over the results—despite a dialogue sequence tacked onto the end of the silent film—but *Picture Play* did note that "Carol Lombard, a very pretty blonde, is worth watching."

Some forty-seven years later, Eddie Quillan would recall Lombard most fondly, commenting that she was full of fun and particularly well-liked by the crew working on *Show Folks*. Already Carol's unpretentious, no-nonsense attitude was endearing her to colleagues in the movie world.

Her next Pathé effort was a "prestige" picture for the studio, an adaptation of Sidney Howard's play, *Ned McCobb's Daughter* (1928), starring Irene Rich, Theodore Roberts, and Robert Armstrong. Carol had a relatively small but decent role as a waitress wooed by unscrupulous bootlegger George Callahan (George Baeraud), who plies her with jewelry bought with money stolen from father-in-law Ned McCobb's ferry business. *The New York Times* summed up the film as "worthy" with "some excellent dramatic passages." Released at the end of 1928, it came at a time when silent features caused few

ripples in Hollywood, and Lombard's work went largely unnoticed in the one town where it counted most.

While Pathé geared up for sound, Carol returned to Mack Sennett's for another two-reel comedy, *Matchmaking Mamas* (1929). It reunited her with Sally Eilers and marked her final silent-film appearance.

Talkies took Hollywood by storm, and ruined many a budding career. But Carol's voice was natural and likeable, and it caused no problems at Pathé, where she

HIGH VOLTAGE (1929). With William Boyd

was cast with William Boyd in an all-talkie called *High Voltage* (1929). The film was anything but electrifying, spinning the tale of a small group of bus passengers stranded in a snowbound church. Lombard played a woman being taken to prison by Sheriff Owen Moore. During their tense vigil, both Moore and telephone lineman Boyd (actually a convict on the run) find themselves falling in love with her. In the end, Boyd and Lombard decide to pay their debt to society and resume their romance afterward.

High Voltage offered one consolation to Carol: there was nowhere to go but up. Her next film, *Big News* (1929), co-starred her in a production that anticipated the rash of early-thirties newspaper melodramas. As the neglected wife of hard-drinking, hard-working reporter Robert Armstrong, Lombard did well, and enjoyed working with director Gregory La Cava, who was to figure importantly in her evolving career several years later.

Armstrong and Lombard were reunited in *The Racketeer* (1930), which cast her as a young woman torn between her love for a struggling violinist and her obligation to a smooth-talking gangster (Armstrong) who subsidizes the musician's career. Rather standard fare, the film nevertheless garnered Lombard some good reviews, with

BIG NEWS (1929). With Robert Armstrong

THE RACKETEER (1930). With Robert Armstrong

Film Daily calling it "her best work to date. In fact this is the first opportunity she has had to prove that she has the stuff to go over. With looks, and a good trouping sense, she also has the personality."

This was, oddly enough, Lombard's last film for Pathé. Biographer Larry Swindell indicates that while the official reason for the studio dropping Lombard was a general cutback, she later learned that new contractee Constance Bennett had ordered her firing since she resembled her too closely.

Leaving Pathé was a mixed blessing for Carol Lombard. She had started to feel at home there, even though her roles, and her films, were mediocre at best. But in truth, Pathé had little to offer her, and in view of the company's imminent demise (and merger with RKO), she was probably better off on her own.

Nineteen-thirty was not the most fortuitous time to be freelancing in Hollywood. Talkie panic hadn't yet settled down, and an "unknown quantity" was liable to remain unknown while studios rushed to test their own silent stars, as well as imported Broadway thespians, for sound.

But Lombard was no longer an unknown. While hardly a star, she *did* have some background and a handful of films to her credit as leading lady and second-lead. She was also well-known from Hollywood social life, and had made many friends since she first stepped onto the Cocoanut Grove dance floor in the mid-twenties.

A job from Cecil B. DeMille the year before in his first talkie, *Dynamite*, had fallen through after a short time because the director reportedly didn't think Carol took her role seriously enough. But this hadn't really done her any harm in casting circles.

After leaving Pathé, her first job came at Fox, for ex-boss Winnie Sheehan. He cast her in the "other woman" role in *The Arizona Kid* (1930), the sequel to 1929's smash hit *In Old Arizona*, starring Warner Baxter (again) in the role of the Cisco Kid, here renamed The Arizona Kid. Baxter's leading lady was Mona Maris (as Lorita), but in the story he falls for a glamorous visitor from the East, Virginia Hoyt (Lombard), who entrances the Kid

PROGRESS AT PARAMOUNT

with her beauty and sophistication. It turns out, though, that Virginia and her "brother" (Theodore von Eltz) are actually man and wife, a con team who learn about the Kid's secret mine and attempt to plunder it—all, of course, to no avail. The Kid ends up with Lorita, and Virginia ends up brotherless.

For Lombard it was a slightly absurd role, but one which she enjoyed, since it was like nothing she'd ever done before. Reviewers and audiences liked the film, but more than a few questioned the wisdom of her casting.

After *The Arizona Kid*, Carol lined up another assignment at Paramount, co-starring in *Safety in Numbers* (1930) with the studio's boyish leading man, Buddy Rogers. The plot for this amiably silly movie has Rogers about to inherit a pile of money; worried that he's naive, his uncle sends him to New York ("just across the river from America") and installs him in an apartment with three world-weary girls from the *Follies*, who teach him about "life." Lombard doesn't have the lead, nor does she win Rogers in the end (that honor goes to Kathryn Crawford), but she does get to talk-sing one amorous song, "(Young Man) You Appeal to Me," with a line that declares, "you have the key to my ignition." She

THE ARIZONA KID. (1930). With Warner Baxter

also gets to spend most of her on-screen moments wearing flimsy negligees, which she does with finesse.

Safety in Numbers was the first of twenty-two films Lombard was to make for Paramount under a seven-year contract she won on the strength of her initial work at the studio, as well as the general impression she made on studio executives.

Her second film at Paramount was an auspicious one, with a good role, but it was all too typical of the stiff early-talkies that could have easily destroyed her career. *Fast and Loose* (1930) was adapted from Avery Hopwood's play *The Best People* by the upcoming

screenwriter Preston Sturges, and cast Carole as a friendly showgirl who attracts the attention of Henry Wadsworth, scion of a prominent New York family, while his sister (Miriam Hopkins) falls in love with a car mechanic (Charles Starrett). The class-conscious parents are naturally dismayed, until they learn that the two working-class young people have more common sense and dignity than their own children!

It's really Miriam Hopkins' film—a dubious distinction, since *Fast and Loose* is so stilted and unrewarding—but it did nothing for *either* actress' stock, since the film was a box-office *and* a critical flop.

Still, *Fast and Loose* has earned a niche in film history—as

SAFETY IN NUMBERS (1930). With Roscoe Karns, Kathryn Crawford, and Josephine Dunn

FAST AND LOOSE (1930). With Frank Morgan, Herbert Yost, Ilka Chase, and David Hutcheson

Hopkins' screen debut, as an early scenario by Preston Sturges, and, as the film in which Carol became Carol*e* Lombard. Apparently it was an accident, pure and simple, but the actress liked it and adopted it as the permanent spelling.

Paramount was suffering from financial woes in the early thirties, and was committed to a slate of sixty-odd feature-film releases per year—more than one new film available to theaters every week! To those who find this number staggering, it must be remembered that movies in the thirties were like television today: so much fictional fodder to entertain a mass audience week after week.

David O. Selznick, then assistant to Paramount chieftain Ben Schulberg, recalled in later years the reason the studio was able to churn out so many films on such an unrelenting schedule: "There has never been, to my knowledge, in the history of the businesss, any studio to compete with Paramount at that time for sheer efficiency. There was never such a thing as a writer or director without an assignment for a specific picture that was planned to be made. People were cut off the payroll as soon as their usefulness was ended. Their daily work was checked. No loafing was tolerated. Release dates were never missed, and pictures were turned out once a week."*

* Rudy Behlmer, ed., *Memo From David O. Selznick*, Viking, New York, 1972, p. 18.

At the center of a publicity photograph about 1930

And just like today's television shows, the sixty-two features Paramount produced in 1931 were a varied lot: some big "prestige" pictures, some out-and-out vehicles tailored to the talents of particular stars, and a great many bread-and-butter films: run-of-the-mill comedies, soap operas, musicals, and melodramas, with few big-name stars, but a multitude of familiar and competent players. Carole Lombard fit into the latter pigeonhole, and her films were the bread-and-butter variety.

Feminine stars at Paramount at this time included Marlene Dietrich, Tallulah Bankhead, Nancy Carroll, Ruth Chatterton, Claudette Colbert, Kay Francis, Sylvia Sidney, Miriam Hopkins, Jean Arthur, Frances Dee, Wynne Gibson, and Lilyan Tashman. With a few notable exceptions, the roles assigned to these ladies were interchangeable. In fact, a role was often handed from actress to actress, subject to their availability or fondness for the part. As indentured servants, they were expected to do films assigned to them, but it was not uncommon for loud objections to be raised and assignments switched.

Understanding all of this is essential to any examination of Carole Lombard's career over the next few years. Knowing what we do about her talent, beauty, and vivacity, it's frustrating to see a drab, lifeless Lombard in a succession of films that range from dull to mediocre. But the same might be said for the early-thirties appearances of Jean Arthur and Claudette Colbert, who, like Lombard, didn't truly blossom as personalities until the middle of the decade.

The Lombard Look was as buried as the Lombard Personality at this time. In most of her Paramount films, she was wedged into the Hollywood mold of current fashion: flat, marcelled hair and impossibly heavy eye makeup. This did not obscure her beauty, but it certainly didn't promote it either. She looked better in some of her Sennett films, and it would take several years for the magnificent Lombard face to reflect its true beauty.

As for the films themselves, 1931 led off with a light comedy based on the well-known stage play, *It Pays to Advertise*, which had been filmed before in 1919. She was co-featured with boy-next-door Norman Foster, as the secretary who helps an ambitious young man promote a fictitious soap product, in order to best his businessman father at his own game. The cast was bolstered by Paramount stalwarts Richard "Skeets" Gallagher, wisecracker par excellence, and Eugene Pallette, blusterer cum laude. Also in the cast was Louise Brooks, a beautiful silent-film star who hadn't

IT PAYS TO ADVERTISE (1931). With Norman Foster

played the Hollywood game, moved to Europe for several years, and paid the price when she tried to return; in the thirties, she was grateful for even minor roles such as this one.

Carole's next film paired her with William Powell, and set off the sparks that led to their marriage later that year.

On-screen, *Man of the World* was his picture, not hers. Powell plays a once-respected American reporter living in exile in Paris, and earning his keep by blackmailing thick-witted tourists from home. His latest conquest is wealthy Guy Kibbee, but his con-game is so smooth that the victim doesn't even realize Powell is behind the extortion. Kibbee introduces Powell to his beautiful niece (Lombard), who's in Paris with her fiancé (Lawrence Gray). When Gray leaves on business for several days, Powell escorts Lombard around Paris, and they quickly fall in love. Naturally, it's too good to last, and Powell's past catches up with him; Lombard goes home with her fiancé, and Powell skips town with his moll, Wynne Gibson.

With a cerebral script by Herman Mankiewicz and a surprisingly effective Parisian atmosphere, *Man of the World* is offbeat and entertaining. Its sophistication is flawlessly conveyed by suave William Powell, whose part and performance are so strong that they make Lombard seem doubly dull. She's serviceable, but no more, and her major asset in this film is an eye-catching array of gowns.

This wasn't exactly corn-pone entertainment for the masses, but *Man of the World* was successful enough to inspire another Powell vehicle with a not-dissimilar title, *Ladies' Man*. Herman Mankiewicz again wrote the screenplay, from a story by Rupert Hughes, and like *Man of the World*, *Ladies' Man* emerged a truly offbeat production.

Curiously, Carole was demoted in this second film, from leading lady to second-lead (and third or fourth in importance to the plot). She plays the daughter of a woman (Olive Tell) who's the latest matron to fall in love with suave gigolo James Darricott (Powell); in spite of herself, Lombard also falls in love with the debonair Darricott. Meanwhile, Darricott experiences *real* love for the first time, with Norma Page (Kay Francis). His sordid past cannot be ignored, however, for Tell's husband (Gilbert Emery) learns of Darricott's dalliances with his wife *and* daughter and goes to his penthouse for revenge. In the fight that ensues, Darricott topples over the railing to his death on the sidewalk below.

Ladies' Man is another odd and downbeat picture, though lacking the sophistication and occasional sparkle of its predecessor. But it

MAN OF THE WORLD (1931). With William Powell

LADIES' MAN (1931). With William Powell

does give Lombard some pearly moments, including a drunk scene in which she confronts Powell at a nightclub and follows him home; there she becomes frantic, throwing herself at Powell, threatening to kill herself but then changing her mind, and swearing vengeance for his callous attitude toward her. She carries this off quite well, and even earns closeups throughout the film—but she's still the ingenue, taking a back-seat to Kay Francis.

Carole triumphed in real life, however, by marrying William Powell on June 26, 1931, some weeks after *Ladies' Man* was released to the theaters.

Powell had been married before, but was long estranged from his wife, and he obtained a divorce so he could marry Lombard. She was more than seventeen years his junior, as different from him in taste and personality as possible. But they fell in love, nevertheless.

William Powell was much the same off-screen as he appeared to be in his starring vehicles: suave, witty, intellectual, and impeccably well-dressed. He was as staid as Carole was spontaneous, and it seemed an unlikely match. In fact, it *was*, but they only discovered this for themselves after being married.

Meanwhile, back at the studio, Carole continued to appear in a succession of ordinary pictures. *Up Pops the Devil* was a quickly made, quickly forgotten tale of a stubborn young man (Norman Foster) who tries out role-reversal with his dedicated wife: he stays home during the day, trying to write the Great American Novel, while she earns regular money working as a chorus girl. Doggedly routine, the film even cheats us out of a glimpse of Carole "doing her stuff" onstage, annoyingly fading to black every time we're about to watch her dance. The film, incidentally, was remade in 1938 with Bob Hope and Shirley Ross as *Thanks for the Memory*; due to literary rights, neither picture is available for television or rental, but it's no great loss.

I Take This Woman gave Carole some lovely dresses to wear, but little else. Gary Cooper was the official star, playing an unpretentious cowboy who falls in love with a snobbish New York debutante visiting her father's ranch. Any ten-year-old could fill in the rest of the story's details; the tired formula was reworked much better as a comedy for Gary Cooper seven years later, in *The Cowboy and the Lady*.

I Take This Woman did win Carole an outstanding and perceptive review from *Variety*: "A few more performances like this from Carole Lombard and Paramount will have a new star on its list. But some better talkers than *I Take This Woman* would ease the climb . . . (She) climbs on top of the part

Lombard, circa 1932

and becomes a distinct personality. She has a face that photographs from all angles and in her playing never falters. Miss Lombard ought to advance rapidly from this point."

But Paramount wasn't listening. Their "rising" young star was then cast in another potboiler, *No One Man* (1932). The title of the film is explained by Carole, a spoiled socialite who believes a perfect marriage impossible because "no one man could have *all* the virtues." Appropriately, she fluctuates between solid, respectable doctor Paul Lukas (a New York gynecologist) and irresponsible playboy Ricardo Cortez (who tells her after an outdoor embrace, "The moon *needs* a pair of lovers like us."). No one man—or woman—in the audience was terribly excited about this trifle.

It was followed by yet another turkey, *Sinners in the Sun* (1932), co-starring Chester Morris. This time, Carole is a model and Morris is a chauffeur; they're in love, but money stands in the way of their marriage. Eventually, each one marries a wealthy partner but regrets the mistake, and after their respective divorces, they come

UP POPS THE DEVIL (1931). With Norman Foster

1316-68

I TAKE THIS WOMAN (1931). With Gary Cooper

NO ONE MAN (1932). With Ricardo Cortez

together again, poor but happy. Of the capable co-stars, *Variety* wrote, "They are called upon to make believable a script which sinks from its own weight."

Lombard then suffered the supreme indignity: loan-out from Paramount to Columbia Pictures, still smarting from a Poverty Row image. Columbia boss Harry Cohn was determined to break that image in Hollywood, and eventually he had the last laugh on the other studios. Stars and directors who were loaned to his studio seemed to do *better* work there than they did at their home base! And it was certainly true for Carole Lombard.

She made five films for Columbia during the next three years, and while only one was of the first-rank, the others were at least as good as her Paramount vehicles, and several were decidedly better. What's more, Carole was a *star* at Columbia, not merely a leading lady.

Her first loan-out film, *Virtue* (1932), co-starred young Pat O'Brien. It was directed by former comedian Edward Buzzell, and written by the talented Robert Riskin, who was to become one of the great loves in Lombard's life. The story itself was stock (a prostitute goes straight, marries a cabdriver, is haunted by her past, and finally redeemed) but smoothly handled.

Her second Columbia film, *No*

SINNERS IN THE SUN (1932). With Chester Morris

More Orchids (1932), presented an equally standard plot: Lombard wants to marry Lyle Talbot, and her banker father (Walter Connolly) is all for it, until a financial crunch makes it necessary for her to go along with a "planned" marriage to a foreign Prince. In a bizarre wrap-up, Connolly commits suicide so that his life-insurance money will both save his failing bank and prevent his daughter from having to go ahead with the loveless nuptials.

Perhaps the most significant outcome of *No More Orchids* was that Carole worked with an amiable and talented director named Walter Lang, who in turn was introduced to Carole's advisor and confidante, Madalynne Fields; they later married, and Carole was the godmother of their son. Lang recalled, "We had so much fun, and the picture turned out so well, that the friendship grew from there till her death . . . (she was) a lovely person, a great person." He later directed her at Universal in *Love Before Breakfast*.

Like *Virtue*, *No More Orchids* was surprisingly well received—and like its predecessor, was also a good-looking picture. Joseph Walker had photographed the first, and Joseph August the second of Lombard's Columbia outings. Both ace cameramen, they worked within Columbia's prescribed boundaries to make the productions look as good as possible.

Even better-looking was Carole's next effort for Paramount, *No Man of Her Own* (1932). For the first time in several months, she was working on her home lot; and this time her leading man was on loan from MGM. His name: Clark Gable.

VIRTUE (1932). With Pat O'Brien

NO MORE ORCHIDS (1932). With Lyle Talbot

In one of those frequent Hollywood ironies, Gable and Lombard—the perfect couple—made only one film together, and that one early in their respective careers, before they were superstars or even established personalities . . . and long before they ever fell in love.

Some years later, Lombard told Garson Kanin, "We made a picture together for Wesley Ruggles, over at Paramount. Pretty good picture, too. *No Man of Her Own*. And we worked together and did all kinds of hot love scenes and everything. And I never got any kind of tremble out of him at all. You know, he was just the leading man. So what? A hunk of meat. Of course, it didn't help that I was on my ear about a different number at the time."

Screen billing on the film's main title told the story of what was what in 1932. "CLARK GABLE in NO MAN OF HER OWN—with Carole Lombard and Dorothy Mackaill." Even though Paramount was her stamping ground, and she had certainly established herself, Carole was still not a star in the studio's mind. Gable, however, had skyrocketed to success in one short year.

He had come from the stage, after one earlier attempt to crash Hollywood in the twenties, when he won a handful of minor appearances and walk-ons in various films, looking wide-eyed

CAROLE MEETS CLARK

and collegiate. His return to the stage solidified his acting credentials, however, and his performance in a Los Angeles production of the grim prison drama *The Last Mile* brought him back to Hollywood in high style. He won film roles on the strength of the play, but they took their cue from that show and cast him as heavies and tough-guys. Coincidentally, Gable made his film debut at Pathé, not long after Carole left the studio, with her former leading man, William Boyd. The picture was *The Painted Desert*.

At Warner Brothers and then at MGM, however, it was discovered that Gable had more than villainy to offer. His rough manner was attractive to women, and within months, Gable was an MGM star, appearing opposite Joan Crawford, Norma Shearer, Marion Davies, Greta Garbo, and Jean Harlow. The large ears which had annoyed certain casting directors didn't seem to bother the ladies at all. And his unaffected manliness made him popular with male moviegoers as well.

It all happened so suddenly that Gable couldn't believe it, and he kept repeating the New York actors' motto, "Don't buy anything you can't put on the Chief," referr-

NO MAN OF HER OWN (1932). With Clark Gable

ing to the cross-country train that would take him home after the bubble burst in Hollywood.

So much in demand was young Mr. Gable that Paramount was happy to acquire his services in return for those of Bing Crosby, whom MGM wanted for a Marion Davies picture. The exchange was made, and Gable checked in at Paramount for *No Man of Her Own*.

In the film he plays "Babe" Stewart, an ultra-smooth con-man with a poker-playing racket. When it gets too hot for him in New York, he decides to leave town for a while, and blindly picks the town of Glendale off a list of railroad destinations.

Glendale is a sleepy little community with nothing to offer Babe—except the acquaintance of beautiful Connie Randall (Lombard), the town librarian. She's immediately attracted to him, but feels at first that it's wrong to let him know it. She secretly longs to have someone take her away from her dull home town, and when the opportunity presents itself, she goes after Babe, prodding him to gamble on *her*, with a flip of a silverpiece determining whether or not they should marry. "I never go back on a coin," says the unruffled Babe, and with that, they are wed.

They return to Babe's apartment in New York, but Connie has no knowledge of what he does for a living—and isn't aware of his reputation. (Earlier in the film, he tells amorous accomplice Dorothy Mackaill, "I'm a hit and run guy—never going to have to comb any dame out of *my* hair!") Connie shames her husband into going to an office and putting in working hours, and eventually, when she learns about his crooked poker games, manages to make him feel ashamed of that as well.

He leaves her for three months, on the pretense of taking a business trip to South America, but in reality, he's given himself up to "copper" Collins (J. Farrell MacDonald), who has agreed to erase Babe's record in return for a ninety-day jail stretch on Blackwell's Island.

Connie is fooled for a while by phony telegrams from South America, but eventually she catches on, and Babe's friend and partner Vane (Grant Mitchell) tells her that Babe "wanted to get the mud off his shoes." Then Babe's old flame Kay (Mackaill) arrives, and tries to smear him with Connie by telling her the same story—but Connie is neither surprised, nor put off, by her. Kay has to admit that she's impressed with Connie, and leaves in gracious defeat.

Babe comes home, unaware that the beans have been spilled, and laden with bogus souvenirs of South America, greets his wife, ready to turn over a new leaf and

NO MAN OF HER OWN (1932). With Clark Gable

spend the rest of his life as her devoted husband.

No Man of Her Own is pretty obvious fare, but it's made pleasant and engaging by its brisk pace and capable cast. Gable is bright and believable as the gambler-gone-good, and is ably abetted by Grant Mitchell, Dorothy Mackaill, J. Farrell MacDonald, and the supporting players.

Lombard has little opportunity to invest anything special in her role—which paints her as just too good to be true—but she's quite capable, and very beautiful. Some of her scenes with Gable *do* have a certain sparkle; made before the restrictive Hollywood Production Code, the film features a morning-after-honeymoon sequence in a Pullman car that's sexy and winning, and a few risqué moments, as when Gable gets librarian Lombard to search for books on a ladder so he can peer up her skirt. There's also a totally gratuitous (but delightful) scene in which Carole, staying at a mountain cabin, runs to answer the phone wearing only the briefest of lingerie. (This shot was memorable enough to be used in Saul Turell's compilation film, *The Love Goddesses*, thirty years later.)

Reinforcing his tough guy-lover image, but softening it with charming comedy, Gable came off well in

Clark Gable at home in 1932

No Man of Her Own. Variety claimed, "Gable is close to the whole picture himself as a swank card-gyp who hits the trail heavy for the women. The review added, "In his supporting company, from Miss Lombard down, Paramount hasn't cheated him at all."

The New York Times wrote, "Miss Lombard and Mr. Gable are amusing and competent players. Between them they keep a rather unusual sort of melodrama bustling along at a lively clip and sustain a pleasing illusion of handsome romantics and dashing humor."

None of the reviewers mentioned one aspect of the film that is highly noticeable today. Gable seems to have been fitted for new false teeth just before shooting, because he purses his lips incessantly, in an unbecoming gesture one is hard-pressed to recall from any of his other films.

The strengths, impact, and outcome of the picture were vividly described by its director, Wesley Ruggles, many years later, talking to Larry Swindell: "When we ran it off for the first time I was damned impressed, though nobody else seemed to be. I loved the first part of the picture—it had a lot of realistic comedy crammed in, and this was exactly what we had decided to work for. Carole and Clark both knew exactly what they were doing. Clark was a damn sight better light comedian than he ever got credit for being. Yet I thought Carole was the revelation. Somebody complained that she didn't seem to be acting, which was one hell of a complaint. Because it didn't *look* like acting, it was so damn natural. Look at the picture today. It's dated, but her work hasn't. She's very fresh. She's playing straight, but using comedy technique, too. Those idiots who'd taken over the studio—they couldn't even see that. Well, the critics didn't see it either. She was wonderful, but it just passed by."*

* Larry Swindell, *Screwball*, William Morrow, 1975, p. 122.

After *No Man of Her Own*, it was back to the usual grind at Paramount, with four film assignments filling 1933—as well as a significant turn of events in Carole's private life.

From Hell to Heaven was one of a rash of pictures which attempted to sponge off the huge success of MGM's *Grand Hotel*. Like Warner Brothers' *Union Depot*, this one gathered a variety of "colorful" characters in one setting, intertwining their stories with a touch of comedy, romance and melodrama. The emphasis is on top-billed Lombard, a wealthy divorcee who attends an important horse race, as the owner of one of the prime contenders, and tries to rekindle her affair with Cuff Billings (Sidney Blackmer), a bookie. The racetrack hotel provides an opportunity to meet the sundry other characters who fill in the episodic story: Jack Oakie, Adrienne Ames, David Manners, et al. The film was just another filler for Lombard.

Supernatural, despite its alluring title, took Carole down another notch. Directed by Victor Halperin, who had caused a stir with his independently made *White Zombie* (starring Bela Lugosi) the year before, this ambitious and offbeat film fell sadly short of its mark. The story involves an heiress (Lombard) who is duped by a so-called medium (Alan Dinehart) who promises to establish contact with

BACK TO THE GRIND

her dead brother. Her body is then "possessed" by the spirit of an executed murderess seeking revenge on the phony medium.

Intriguing in its storyline, *Supernatural* disappoints in its execution, which is murky and unsatisfying. Lombard does her best in a somewhat challenging role, with young Randolph Scott as nominal leading man, but, in the words of *Motion Picture Herald*, "The too obvious effort to appear mystical, mysterious, and weird causes (the film) at times to descend of its own weight to something approaching absurdity."

No such absurdity crept into Carole's next movie, *The Eagle and the Hawk*. A superb anti-war film, its only problem was that it offered Lombard so little to do. Written by John Monk Saunders (remembered for *Wings* and other World War One aviation sagas), the story focuses on Fredric March as a flyer who becomes increasingly embittered by the war—the killing of mere boys, the seeming sport of aerial combat, and the false glory accorded "heroes" like himself. His feelings become so intense that he is given a temporary leave in order to get away from war for a while; in London, he meets a beautiful woman (Lombard), sympathetic to his problems and undemanding after their night of love.

FROM HELL TO HEAVEN (1933). With Sidney Blackmer

SUPERNATURAL (1933). With Alan Dinehart

THE EAGLE AND THE HAWK (1933). With Fredric March

Director Mitchell Leisen later told David Chierichetti, "Carole was a little younger here than in the other pictures I did with her, and I think the shots of her leaning against the mantle, watching the agony March is going through were particularly beautiful. Carole was already an established leading lady, and it was unheard of for somebody of her stature to accept such a small part, but I asked her to do it and she agreed."*

Some reviewers weren't so pleased, however, as indicated by this comment from *Variety*: "Strictly a formula story of the

Royal Flying Corps by the man who wrote *Wings*, with a laboriously dragged in romantic bit to get a feminine star's (Lombard's) name on the program. But it takes more than fifty or sixty feet of sex stuff to make love interest. It might have been left out . . . Carole Lombard contributes little in spite of sincere playing."

Other reports were not so unflattering, and in recent years *The Eagle and the Hawk* has earned a well-deserved reputation for its solid plot and fine performances. Sadly, when the film was reissued in 1939, some of its more potent scenes were cut or altered to conform with then-current feelings about sex—and war.

* David Chierichetti, *Hollywood Director*, Curtis Books, New York, 1973, p. 59.

*BRIEF MOMENT (1933). With Gene Raymond and
Monroe Owsley*

During a dormant filmmaking period, Carole established residence in Nevada in order to obtain a divorce from William Powell. Although the official charge was extreme cruelty, there had never been any cruelty in the marriage—just problems of compatability based on their separate and busy careers, as well as conflicting personalities. It was often said that she had become more serious, and he more lively, during their union, partly to accommodate each other, partly from the influence they exerted on each other. Whatever the reasons, there was no venom in their divorce, and no alimony. They remained good friends and even co-starred again in a film, quite memorably, and appeared on radio as a team.

Back in Hollywood, Lombard returned to Columbia Pictures for an average outing called *Brief Moment*, based on a play by S. N. Behrman. As a nightclub singer who marries (and tries to reform) spoiled, wealthy Gene Raymond, Lombard couldn't overcome a routine script, but she looked exquisite, and took note of the cameraman's name: Ted Tetzlaff. She later insisted on Tetzlaff as her photographer at Paramount, and took him with her when she shuttled from Paramount to Universal and Warner Brothers.

It was the costumes, however, and not the photography, that lent Carole distinction in her next film, *White Woman*. True to the title of this programmer, she appeared in the middle of a jungle dressed in a chic, sexy, white-on-white sheath outfit, with an eye-opening slit down the front, plus a white bandana and a' white, wide-brimmed hat. This, and her world-weary rendition of two Gordon-Revel tunes ("Yes, My Dear," and "A Gentleman and a Scholar") in a cabaret setting, were the main points of interest in *White Woman*, which cast her as an entertainer who marries coarse, sadistic plantation owner Charles Laughton to avoid deportation from Malaya.

The picture somewhat belies the studio's ongoing claim that "if it's a Paramount Picture, it's the best show in town." In fact, one angry theater-owner from North Carolina wrote to *Motion Picture Herald* about *White Woman*, "This is one of the worst pictures we have ever put before the public. Paramount should be ashamed to put such trash off on the poor exhibitors and make them pay for it. No story, no entertainment, and terrible recording."

Even while *White Woman* was garnering this reaction, Paramount was starting to publicize what looked like its first sure hit of 1934: *Bolero*.

Once more, Carole was taking back-seat to a male star, with George Raft's name above the title

59

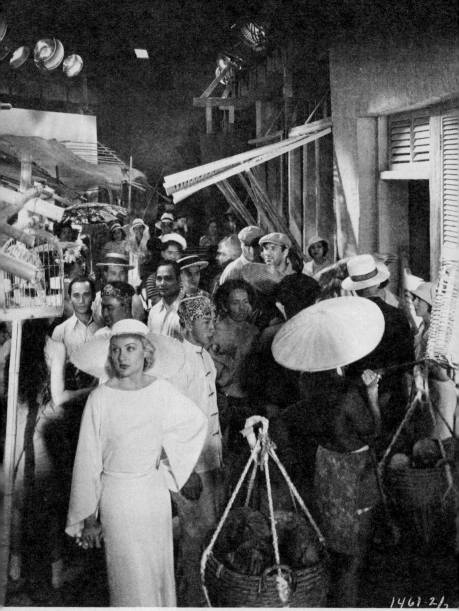

WHITE WOMAN (1933). On the set of the film

BOLERO (1934). With George Raft

BOLERO (1934). With Ray Milland

and hers below, next to those of fan-dancer Sally Rand and beautiful brunette Frances Drake. But in spite of this, *Bolero* gave her a fine opportunity on-screen and a successful picture at last.

The film opens in 1910, with Raft as Raoul De Baere, a mine worker determined to leave that job and make a name for himself as a dancer. Hooted off the stage in an amateur show, he tells his brother (William Frawley) that nothing's going to stand in his way. After enjoying some measure of success at a local beer garden, he goes to Paris and teams with a beautiful girl named Leona (Frances Drake);

eventually they become the rage of Paris as nightclub dancers. But Leona isn't satisfied with just a business relationship; she's stuck on Raoul and is starting to cause complications.

Enter Helen Hathaway (Lombard), a former Ziegfeld girl who's just as determined as Raoul. She lays her case on the line: she wants to be his partner, has no romantic inclinations, and hopes to attract enough attention to snag herself a rich husband. Raoul is skeptical, but when Leona pulls another of her temper tantrums, he leaves her and accepts Helen as his new partner. Taken with her great beauty, he warns her, "If I ever fall for you, say no!"

Raoul and Helen are a huge success, but he finds himself increasingly concerned about her private life. When handsome Lord Coray (Ray Milland) is highly attentive, he becomes jealous, and keeping her word, she reminds them of their pact, even though she too feels a growing affection for her partner.

Raoul's career reaches its zenith with the opening of his swank nightclub in Paris, but the triumph is marred by the outbreak of World War One. He interrupts his dance with Helen to declare his allegiance to France and his intention to enlist the following day, bringing him cheers from the packed audience. But backstage he confesses that it's all a publicity stunt; this disappointment convinces Helen to leave and marry Lord Coray.

Shocked, and shamed by her rebuff, Raoul goes through with his enlistment, and serves bravely during the war, emerging in 1918 with a weakened heart. More determined than ever, he ignores his doctor's warning and returns to his club. On opening night, his natural anxiety is heightened when his

WE'RE NOT DRESSING (1934). With Ethel Merman and Leon Errol

new partner Annette (Sally Rand) shows up late—and drunk. Raoul's brother/manager spots Helen in the audience with her husband and prevails upon her to give Raoul his one dream, to open that night with the Bolero. She agrees, and together they dazzle the audience with their breathtaking performance.

Returning to their dressing rooms, they prepare for an encore, the applause still thundering outside; Helen tells him from the next room how happy she is for him, although he must understand that it's their last dance together. And indeed it is, for Raoul has fallen to the floor, dead. The applause of the unknowing audience continues as Raoul's brother speaks the phrase that had piloted the dancer ever upward through his career: "He was too good for this joint."

Although it sounds corny, *Bolero* is fine entertainment and good storytelling. Handsomely produced, the film shows both Raft and Lombard to good advantage. She's stunning in her very first scene, wearing an elaborately plumed costume, and beautifully photographed by Leo Tover. Her characterization of the hard-edged but vulnerable showgirl allows her to use her personality in a way most earlier parts had not, and her dance scenes with Raft are great fun.

As for the "Bolero" finale, using the music of Maurice Ravel, there is some reason to doubt that Raft and Lombard actually participated in the sequence. It is recorded that after Wesley Ruggles finished the picture, Mitchell Leisen was called in to reshoot this one sequence. An experienced hoofer, Raft was never noted as an adagio dancer, and the leaps and twirls of the Bolero seem beyond his range. The entire sequence is filmed in long-shot, with the couple's faces cleverly obscured by mood lighting, and closeups neatly intercut to give the illusion that they are indeed dancing this number. In *Rumba*, made the following year, the popular dance team of Veloz and Yolanda were actually credited for doing the Raft-Lombard finale, a much less ambitious number than this. It is reasonable, then, to assume that doubles must have been used here, although it is still possible for Carole to have done her part, with an able partner, as she *was* a fine dancer. Whatever the truth, it remains a well-kept secret, especially by Raft, who regards *Bolero* as one of his favorite pictures.

Raft also cherishes the memory of his co-star. "I truly loved Carole Lombard," he told biographer Lewis Yablonsky. "She was the greatest girl that ever lived and we were the best of pals." It has been intimated that they were more than just "pals," but their liaison was not a lasting one.

WE'RE NOT DRESSING (1934). As Doris Worthington

Another actor who was impressed by his leading lady in *Bolero* was Ray Milland. It was his first film for Paramount, and a big break in his career. One vivid memory for him was the filming of Sally Rand's famous fan dance, a featured spot in the movie. He recalled, "Everybody on the lot piled into Stage Five to watch it, including some characters who made it over the wall from RKO. I was sitting at a ringside table and never felt a twinge. Perhaps it was because my table companion was Carole Lombard, a smashing girl, a true original, and a hell of an actress. When she was annoyed, her language was that of a stevedore. She loved practical jokes and could tell a bawdy story with the best of them. In any company, her taste was impeccable."*

Milland was able to reaffirm his opinion, since he was immediately cast in Carole's next picture, *We're Not Dressing* (1934). A frothy musical comedy loosely based on James Barrie's *The Admirable Crichton*, it gave Carole official "leading-lady" status, but pitted her against such strong screen personalities as Bing Crosby, George Burns and Gracie Allen, Ethel Merman, and Leon Errol. For all her beauty and charm, Carole Lombard is the person one remembers

* Ray Milland, *Wide-Eyed in Babylon*, William Morrow, New York, 1974, p. 164.

least from *We're Not Dressing*, although she does inspire two of Crosby's all-time best songs, "May I" and "Love Thy Neighbor." The plot, such as it is, concerns a crew member (Crosby) on wealthy Doris Worthington's (Lombard's) yacht, who suddenly becomes very important to the formerly aloof society guests when their ship is wrecked and they must survive on a deserted island. Love blossoms—with all the appropriate barriers—between lowly Crosby and high-society Lombard, with a happy ending and a lot of gags and songs along the way.

Crosby was delighted with his leading lady and recalled in his autobiography, "Carole could lay tongue to more colorful epithets than any other woman I've ever known, and more than most men. Oddly enough, you never were shocked when she swore. You felt the way you feel when you're with a bunch of men who're fishing or working hard and one of them bangs his thumb with a hammer or gets a fish hook in his pants. Under such circumstances, if they swear nobody pays much attention because they're entitled to let off steam. That was the reaction I had to Carole's profanity. It was good, clean, and lusty. Her swearwords weren't obscene. They were gusty and eloquent. They resounded, and bounced. They had honest zing!

"She had a delicious sense of humor; she was one of the screen's greatest comediennes and, in addition, she was very beautiful. The electricians, carpenters, and prop men all adored her because she was so regular; so devoid of temperament and showboating. The feeling of non-gender camaraderie Carole gave the men who worked with her was a victory of mental attitude over matter, the matter in her case being curvy, blond, and melting. The fact that she could make us think of her as being a good guy rather than as a sexy mama is one of those unbelievable manifestations impossible to explain. All I can say is, that was the way it was."*

Following *We're Not Dressing*, Carole was requested again for loan-out by Columbia.

This time, it was for something special.

* Bing Crosby, *Call Me Lucky*, Simon and Schuster, New York, 1953, pp. 70-71.

Some movie careers are easily diagrammed, while others provide only vague clues to their success or lack of it. Every once in a while, a film, or a specific role, plays such an important part in the shaping of a career that one can easily single it out as the turning point. Such a case is Carole Lombard's performance in *20th Century* (1934).

Second (or third) choice for the film after Gloria Swanson, she was jointly selected by studio chief Harry Cohn and director Howard Hawks to star opposite John Barrymore in the film version of the play by Ben Hecht and Charles MacArthur.

Everyone knew it would be a great opportunity for her, just to be featured with Barrymore. There was no doubt that it was a fine role, either. But few people realized just how good Lombard would be—that she would rate bravos not just for rubbing shoulders with the great Barrymore, but for creating a marvelous performance *herself*.

The story deals with egomaniacal Broadway producer-director Oscar Jaffe, who has found his latest discovery for stardom behind the counter at a department store, and with whimsical inspiration changed her name from Mildred Plotka to Lily Garland. The timid young girl has never been on a stage before, and the great Jaffe sets out to create a star performance from scratch. Rehearsal begins with

THE TURNING POINT

Lily's entrance as a sweet Southern belle, and Jaffe gently observes, "No, my dear, that is the way an *ice-man* would enter the house."

Rehearsals continue, with Jaffe going so far as to diagram her every movement with chalk on the stage floor. Some eight hours later, his veneer of politeness is gone, and he badgers her mercilessly as she continues to speak and move without any semblance of feeling. Finally, she cracks under the strain and cries, telling off the demanding director in no uncertain terms. "I won't crawl on my stomach for *any* man," she wails, truly broken and unhappy. But Jaffe is delighted; her anger has proven that she *does* have some fire within her. "The gold is all there," he declares, "but we must mine it!" In a climactic scene where she must scream, her hesitation causes Jaffe to take desperate measures: at the appropriate moment, he jabs a pin into her behind, producing the required results.

Opening night, her performance is a triumph, and Broadway hails a new star. But Lily is no fool: she knows that she owes it all to Oscar (she's even saved the pin). And *he* knows that *she* knows it.

Three years pass. By now Garland and Jaffe are an established team on Broadway—and offstage as well, where Lily's life has been totally dominated by the mer-

20th CENTURY (1934). With John Barrymore

curial maniac. With every new out-
burst of his, she threatens to leave
him and accept a rival producer's
offer, but he laughs at these claims,
believing that she is still completely
dependent on him. When she finds
out that he's been tapping her
phone and having her investigated,
however, it's the last straw, and she
walks out on Jaffe and accepts a
Hollywood contract.

Without her, Jaffe's career takes
a nosedive. Accompanied by his
much-abused but faithful aides
Oliver Webb (Walter Connolly)
and Owen O'Malley (Roscoe
Karns) he eludes a sheriff's
foreclosure in Chicago and sneaks
onto the 20th Century Limited,
headed for New York. Who should
be on the same train but Lily
Garland, returning from

Hollywood with her dull suitor, George Smith (Ralph Forbes).

At first too proud to do anything, Jaffe is finally convinced that he should try to woo Lily back, in order to save his reputation and ensure a new hit play. She wants no part of him, but the convincing Jaffe won't take no for an answer. There begins a barrage of pleas and hoaxes that drive Lily to the point of hysteria, culminating in a phony heart attack that actually does the trick, getting her to sign a contract in the belief that it's Oscar's dying wish. Before the ink is dry, the "corpse" comes to life, however, reveling in his triumph and rekindling the battling relationship with Lily.

It's impossible to capture the lunacy of *20th Century* on paper. Hecht and MacArthur's daffy situations and dialogue, Barrymore's bravura performance, and the speed of Howard Hawks' direction, are but a few of the reasons the film remains a thirties classic.

Another prominent reason is Carole Lombard.

Her characterization is superb, because it *grows* from the first scene to the last. When we first see her, she's timid and frightened; after eight hours of Oscar Jaffe's grilling she falls apart, in a wonderful, heartfelt scene. This is not played for comedy, but for the humanity of the situation; we truly feel sorry for this girl, because we empathize with her amateur ambitions and recoil at the unsympathetic treatment she receives. Her sincere gratitude toward lecherous Jaffe after opening night is equally touching and geniune.

But three years later, after living with Jaffe, her personality has changed drastically. He has driven her to near-madness, but more intriguingly, he has influenced her personality. She's now assumed some of his theatrical mannerisms and poses, and in the midst of her luxurious apartment, she dramatically intones a mournful comment: "Fame . . . success . . . empty words."

On the 20th Century Limited, she gets sandwiched between the feckless Smith and the flamboyant Jaffe, and in sheer desperation, she sits in place and kicks her legs, crying hysterically like a child.

It's significant, then, that the story comes full-circle when Lily falls for Oscar's hammy performance as a heart-attack victim, this after his other efforts to sign her for a role of Mary Magdalene in his projected Passion Play have failed. She responds to his theatricality because now she's become theatrical herself and has lost her ingenuousness and simple honesty.

20th Century is not really Lombard's film; she's billed below the title, and the dominating performance is Barrymore's. (Of this role

20th CENTURY (1934). With Ralph Forbes

his biographer Gene Fowler wrote, "his talent flared brilliantly (in this) zany masterpiece.")

But she is certainly Barrymore's equal in terms of effectiveness, and the pairing of this "newcomer" with a stage and screen veteran worked magnificently. The film didn't hurt the blossoming career of director Howard Hawks either, and underscored his aptitude for managing frantic comedy which reached its zenith six years later in *His Girl Friday.* It remains one of the director's favorite films, which he considers to have been "three or four years ahead of its time."

In recent years, the film has become an acknowledged classic, "lit up by the radiance of Carole

Lombard's femininity," according to famed film curator Henri Langlois, and "the film which first established Carole Lombard as the finest comedienne of the thirties," according to film critic/scholar Andrew Sarris.

But more importantly, Lombard's achievement was recognized in 1934—not in *all* quarters, but by enough of the right people to make it matter. *Photoplay* referred to "a fiery talent which few suspected she had," while another fan magazine, *Shadowplay*, tagged her "like no other Lombard you've seen. . . . When you see her, you'll forget the rather restrained and somewhat stilted Lombard of old. You'll see a star blaze out of this scene and that scene, high spots Carole never dreamed of hitting."

Edward Bernds, Columbia's chief sound engineer in the thirties, has this recollection of *20th Century*: "I have never worked on a picture in which the scenes commanded such rapt attention from the crew. But Lombard and Barrymore were dynamite on the set. Anything could happen. We, the crew, were fascinated."

20th Century was not a smash hit. It was too talky and too sophisticated for the mass market, and Columbia's hope that it would follow the success of their blockbuster *It Happened One Night* (released earlier that year) did not come to fruition. Still, it was a moderately successful venture, and as a moral victory for Carole Lombard it was unrivaled.

But when the film was completed, she returned to Paramount and found that nothing much had changed.

20th CENTURY (1934). With John Barrymore

Carole's first assignment back at Paramount should have been something special. It wasn't.

Now and Forever officially co-starred Gary Cooper and Carole Lombard, but co-starred with *them* was the film's *raison d'être*, Shirley Temple, riding the crest of a popularity wave in 1934. Cooper plays a slick jewel thief who works with Lombard in Europe, but returns to the U.S. to clinch a deal whereby his wealthy brother-in-law will pay him a tidy sum for custody of his small daughter. But when Cooper gets to meet the moppet, she charms him and changes his mind; he takes her back to Europe with him and tries to go straight to earn an honest living for his daughter. A blackmailing colleague has different designs on Cooper, however, and forces him to steal again; when Temple finds out, she's heartbroken, and to restore her confidence, Cooper tries to set matters straight, catching a bullet for his trouble, but clearing the decks for eventual happiness with both Temple and Lombard.

Film historian Jeanine Basinger has commented, "*Now and Forever* is a dull, slackly paced film. Cooper and Lombard, two of the most charming players of the 1930s, seem bored with the assignment."

But critics and audiences in 1934 were so enchanted with Shirley Temple (who *is* quite enjoyable) that they forgave the im-

STARRING CAROLE LOMBARD

plausibilities of the plot and overlooked the banality of the two leading roles. This feeling was summed up by Thornton Delehanty in the *New York Post*: "*Now and Forever* may not be a great story—it has its loopholes—but it is expertly contrived to furnish first-rate entertainment." The film was also an early boost for director Henry Hathaway, rapidly rising in the Paramount ranks.

From this undistinguished outing, Carole returned to Columbia for the last time, to do her fifth film of the year (with one more to go). *Lady by Choice* was a follow-up to the studio's hugely successful Frank Capra film of 1933, *Lady for a Day*, with scene-stealing May Robson returning in an Apple Annie-inspired characterization.

Lombard plays Alabam' Lee, a fan-dancer who is periodically arrested for indecent exposure. Her press agent, "Front" O'Malley (Raymond Walburn), cooks up a publicity scheme to draw attention to Alabam', proposing that she "adopt" a mother on Mother's Day. Alabam' goes to an old-age home and chooses Patsy (Robson), a friendly frump she recalls from night court. The "stunt" really brings out the mother in Patsy, however, and soon she's piloting Alabam's career, as well as her love

NOW AND FOREVER (1934). With Gary Cooper and Shirley Temple

life, steering her right in both directions and bringing her together with kind-hearted Johnny Mills (Roger Pryor).

While hardly in the same league with Capra's earlier film, *Lady by Choice* is entirely enjoyable, thanks to a tight script by Jo Swerling (from Dwight Taylor's story), a fine cast ensemble, and handsome photography by Ted Tetzlaff. In the vernacular of the day, Columbia advertising called it "a picture that's just plain, ordinary swell!"

Unfortunately, the film was sold on the association with *Lady for a Day*, and the return of May Robson. Carole got lost in the shuffle, even though she was billed above Robson on the screen and in all advertising. Still, *Variety* took the trouble to note, "Carole Lombard does a lot for the picture. She is forceful, vibrant, and once or twice she shows far greater power than in her previous work."

Lombard's next film was a loan-out as well, and not to lowly Columbia but to the Tiffany of studios, MGM. Unfortunately, Carole's only film for Metro-Goldwyn-Mayer would turn out to be a lemon.

The Gay Bride is an odd mixture of comedy and melodrama, with an uneasiness over which tone should dominate certain scenes. Scripted by Samuel and Bella Spewack from a *Saturday Evening Post* story, it tells of a chorus girl (Lombard) who cons a gangster (Nat Pendleton) into marrying her so that she can realize her ambitions of wealth and power. But this starts a chain reaction as Pendleton is killed by rival Sam Hardy, who in turn is bumped off by ambitious Leo Carrillo. Mixed up in all of this is Pendleton's one-time bodyguard, Chester Morris. And believe it or not, all ends happily (!) with Lombard and Morris in the final clinch.

Some indication of *The Gay Bride*'s level of importance can be assessed by MGM's decision to forego any trade-paper ads for the film. Several reviewers liked the film, but it was gone too quickly to cause any stir (MGM was busy promoting its big Christmas release *David Copperfield*), and it did Lombard no good at all. One of the few theater owners who bothered to write an opinion on the film for *Motion Picture Herald* called it "a good, average picture." Lombard herself later tagged it her all-time worst.

But it wasn't long before another Lombard picture was in release, this one accorded much more fanfare from her home studio, Paramount. Advertising for *Rumba* declared: "The dancing lovers of *Bolero* in a dramatic romance as fiery as the Cuban dance of love itself." That the film was about as fiery as day-old spaghetti didn't bother the promotion men; it was touted as a worthy successor to

LADY BY CHOICE (1934). With May Robson and Walter Connolly

Bolero and the truth be damned. The only improvement over the previous year's film was that this time Carole's name appeared above the title along with George Raft's.

The "story" of *Rumba* pits ambitious dancer Raft against slumming socialist Diana Harrison (Lombard), who's vacationing in Havana. Fancying herself in love with him, she offers to subsidize a trip to New York, but he thinks she's just having a laugh at his expense. When he realizes that she really meant it, it's too late.

He finally does come to New York to star in a Broadway show, doing a torrid number called "The Birth of the Rumba," with dancing partner Margo. But in returning to Manhattan he finds his life threatened by former gangland "friends." His decision to go on opening night, despite a threat that he'll be killed onstage, makes front-page news, and backstage that evening, Margo faints from worry. Diana, confessing her love for him once again, goes on instead and their dance is a triumph. Then Raft's press-agent Flash (Lynne Overman) admits that the death-threat was a hoax of his to attract publicity.

Raft and Lombard's climactic number is a letdown, nowhere near the exciting and glamorous routine they (or others) executed in *Bolero*—yet here, the dancing is credited to Veloz and Yolanda.

Similarly, Raft's Latin production number with Margo only induces yawns.

The film has virtually nothing to recommend it except Lombard at her most beautiful, stylishly costumed by Travis Banton and flatteringly photographed by Ted Tetzlaff in his first Paramount assignment. Critics were unimpressed, and since Paramount publicity invited comparison to *Bolero*, everyone noted how inferior the film was to the previous year's success.

Finally, in 1935, Carole Lombard's fortunes changed at Paramount, which still employed her under the contract she had signed in 1930. The brilliant director Ernst Lubitsch was appointed studio production chief, directly responsible for the supervision of filmmaking under the Paramount roof. A longtime Lombard admirer, he now had the opportunity to translate his compliments into action by giving the actress a film worthy of her talents.

The outcome was *Hands Across the Table* (1935), her first real starring vehicle and one of her best films. She lobbied for Mitchell Leisen to direct, and her wish was granted. Theirs was a most happy collaboration. Her leading man was movie newcomer Fred MacMurray, who also worked in great harmony with Lombard, and co-starred with her in three subsequent

THE GAY BRIDE (1934). As Mary

RUMBA (1935). Rehearsing with George Raft

films. Her favorite cameraman, Ted Tetzlaff, worked on the film, and she wore costumes by Travis Banton. Everything was tailored to make *Hands Across the Table* a success, and a personal victory for Carole. It worked.

Our first view of Regi Allen (Carole) is in a subway station, when she and girlfriend Marie Prevost (like Lombard, a former Sennett star) shove their way out of a crowded car on their way to jobs at a fashionable barbershop.

Regi's ambition is to snag a rich husband, having decided that love doesn't really matter. Her wealthy customer Allen Macklyn (Ralph

HANDS ACROSS THE TABLE (1935). With Ralph Bellamy and Joseph Tozer

Bellamy), a former aviator now confined to a wheelchair, is fascinated by her, and comments, "You think a lot about money, don't you?" She bluntly replies, "You've *got* it—you don't have to think about it." In spite of Regi's admitted gold-digging philosophy, Macklyn finds himself falling in love with her.

Then Regi meets Theodore Drew III. His appearance and manner are ordinary, but when she learns that he's the son of the wealthy Drews, she shows him plenty of attention, and is so nervous during his manicure that she cuts his fingers repeatedly. After a date that night, she learns that he's flat broke, and in fact is about to marry for money himself! Having told his fiancée that he's vacationing in Bermuda, he asks Regi if he can stay in her apartment for the rest of the week to avoid problems and save money. She agrees reluctantly, since Ted has no romantic designs on her and agrees with her notion of marrying for money and not for love.

During the week Regi and Ted do their best to deny any feelings between them, but their fondness grows, nonetheless. She even shames him into admitting that perhaps he should be doing something useful with his life besides living off other people's money. When their final night comes, neither one can sleep; in fits and starts they almost express their love, but the moment passes and in the morning Drew is gone.

Regi returns to work and calls on Allen, who's finally ready to propose marriage, when in strides Ted, having told off his fiancée, and now determined to claim Regi for his own. As the helpless Allen looks on, they finally admit their love and run off to be married, Ted promising to "go straight" and get a job.

Labeling *Hands Across the Table* a comedy does it a great disservice. The film has more heart and depth than most of its contemporaries, taking a standard thirties-comedy situation and breathing new life into it with sensitive direction, scripting, and performances.

The closing segment is beautifully orchestrated, and quite moving. In the dark of the night, MacMurray lies restlessly on Lombard's living room sofa, and tries to talk to her about his feelings. She resists stubbornly, fighting a battle within herself. In a strikingly

HANDS ACROSS THE TABLE (1935). With Fred MacMurray

photographed sequence, they walk out onto her rooftop, trying to breathe the air and make some sense of their situation, still maintaining a veneer of aloofness which has characterized their relationship. They return to their beds, but MacMurray can no longer stand it, and silently leaves the apartment (and Lombard) for good. Meanwhile, she relents and walks into the living room to tell him that she loves him—only to find him gone.

Next morning, adding salt to the wound, MacMurray's bitchy fiancée (Astrid Allwyn) sends for manicurist Lombard and—in so many words—calls her a tramp, having discovered her intended's hiding place for the past week. By the time Carole arrives at Bellamy's suite for his appointment, she's shattered. When MacMurray turns up, she doesn't want to see him, but positive persuasion wins out for a happy ending.

This is the Lombard suppressed for so long in drab little soap operas: a warm, winning, full-blown *actress*, with an ability far beyond surface comedy or snappy dialogue.

Amazingly, Fred MacMurray, with just a handful of films behind him, came off equally well in this film. It's ironic that in an early scene of the film, Lombard is supposed to be terribly nervous while manicuring MacMurray, for in real life, *he* was the nervous one. She reportedly kicked him under the table at one point and growled, "Loosen up, you big ape—it isn't going to hurt!" Over the years he has never stopped giving her credit. "I owe so much of that performance and my subsequent career to her. She worked with me on every scene," he told David Chierichetti.

Director Leisen explained, "She had none of what you might call the 'star temperament.' She felt that all the others had to be good or it wouldn't matter how good she was. She got right in there and pitched." Lombard became well-known as one star who participated in conferences on every aspect of her films, from casting to costuming. And as her popularity grew, she learned to use her star-clout to get what she wanted for her pictures.

Hands Across the Table won Carole some well-deserved raves. *Motion Picture Herald* capsulized the trade reaction to the film: "This is the kind of picture which, because little ballyhoo was given it during production stages, has not attracted much attention. Judging by the preview audience reaction, however, the situation is quite likely to be reversed upon presentation and in addition to becoming a widely talked about attraction, the show is potentially promising of exploding into a box-office surprise. *Hands Across the Table*, in appeal

LOVE BEFORE BREAKFAST (1936)
As Kay Colby

of story content, value of substantiating production features, quality of acting and class of direction technique, is of the stuff that makes such an assumption logical. Basically it's semi-sophisticated farce comedy romance geared to mass appeal. As such it includes the essentials which intrigue the intelligentsia and at the same time whip the common garden variety of picture fans into enthusiasm . . . with a performance establishing comedy as Carole Lombard's popular forte."

Hands Across the Table was not a super-production, but it rated as one of Paramount's solid winners in late 1935. And it confirmed the faith that people like Lubitsch and Leisen had had in her.

With nothing immediate to offer, Paramount allowed her to accept a bid from Universal to star (with top billing above the title) in a romantic comedy, *Love Before Breakfast*, with Preston Foster and Cesar Romero.

Going to Universal was not as simple as all that, however. Lombard took with her an entourage, led by cameraman Ted Tetzlaff and costumer Travis Banton (who worked only on her clothes, leaving the rest of the cast to be outfitted by Universal's contract designer Brymer). She also insisted that certain favorite crew members be with her on every picture. George Raft has said, "Carole was wholly

generous, always seeing to it that people she knew or felt sorry for worked as extras. If they didn't work, she wouldn't go on the set."

Among her "unit" was a gaffer named Pat Drew. Mitchell Leisen recalled, "Her pet electrician was flying across the country and the plane crashed somewhere in the vicinity of Kansas City. She personally hired a baggage car and had a bed set up for him sprung on springs to cushion the shocks and make him as comfortable as possible. She got a folding chair and sat up with him all the way back to Los Angeles.

"Word got around town about this and when the train pulled into Union Station downtown, the place was crawling with reporters. Carole took one look from the platform of the train and went into a rage. She called them everything in the book and said if any one of them printed the story she'd never give another interview or let another reporter on any of her sets. 'If one word is printed,' she said, 'God help you all.' She meant it and not one word was printed."*

Carole's kindness was not for show; it was genuine, and even in the Hollywood world of pretense, people knew it, and loved her for it.

Thus, Carole felt at home while doing the picture at Universal. Even the director, Walter Lang,

* *Hollywood Director*, pp. 108-109.

84

was an old acquaintance; he had piloted her Columbia film, *No More Orchids*, several years back.

Unfortunately, the resulting film was hardly worth the trouble. *Love Before Breakfast* is one of those films in which the outcome is so obvious from the first scene that the film must rely entirely on personality and repartée to maintain any degree of interest. Lombard is in fine fettle, and looks glorious, but Preston Foster and Cesar Romero fail to set off the necessary sparks, and the script's gossamer texture shows through. (For the record, Foster plays a millionaire with an eye for Lombard; he contrives to send his rival, and employee, Romero, out of the country, leaving the field clear for himself; complications set in before she realizes that she really does love him.)

Still, the film is innocuously entertaining, and seems to reflect the good time everyone had making it. In a 1971 interview, director Walter Lang recalled for Joel Greenberg, "Carole ... was wonderful to work with. She would stay behind till any hour of the night, and if something bothered us we'd get together at night and go over and get it solved. She was

LOVE BEFORE BREAKFAST (1936). With Preston Foster

always on time and knew her lines, and was a great, great artist."

A climactic sequence at sea had Lombard waterlogged through much of the shooting, but according to Lang, "Carole worked all day; she'd never get out of the water or out of her wet clothes. She'd want to keep on working, till we insisted she get out and have something hot to drink and get into dry clothes—at least to rehearse in until the next plunge. But she was into everything, very much like Katharine Hepburn later on. She had the same interest in the story and the people and the casting and the camera and everything that Hepburn had—and still has."*

Universal advertised *Love Before Breakfast* with an arresting image of the beautiful Carole sporting a black eye. The film was a hit, and happily a boost for her fast-rising career.

When Carole returned to Paramount, it was as a full-fledged star. Her career was in an upward spiral and her popularity reaching its all-time high.

* *Focus on Film*, Issue 18, 1974, pp. 23-24.

As much as a successful career meant to Carole Lombard, it was only *part* of her life. Romance, and fun, were as important to her as any movie role.

The beautiful Carole was never without male companionship, although it was almost always on her terms. A woman who was decidedly fond of sex, she never used it as a tool, like many other actresses who wanted to get ahead. Indeed, it has been speculated that this may be a reason it took so long for her to get the kind of roles she deserved.

After the split with Powell, she emerged even gayer than before, enhancing her reputation as one of the brightest lights on the Hollywood social scene. She was attracted to screenwriter Robert Riskin, and was often rumored to be engaged to him during their two-year, on-again, off-again romance. But the elements never meshed to bring them together on a permanent basis.

Then Carole had a serious affair with crooner Russ Columbo, at one time Bing Crosby's greatest rival. Fan magazines quoted Carole as saying, "His love for me was the kind that rarely comes to any woman." The handsome singer with the amorous voice had just launched a screen career when he and Lombard fell in love. Again, the gossip mills were kept busy predicting engagement and/or nup-

INTERLUDE: LOMBARD OFF-SCREEN

tials, but the speculation was silenced when Columbo, only twenty-six, was killed in a gun accident. Carole wept unashamedly at his funeral.

There were no serious alliances after this tragedy, although fan magazine photographers often found Lombard in the company of eligible Hollywood bachelors, including ex-husband William Powell.

During this time, Carole also acquired a considerable reputation for her zany parties. From the silent days onward she was known as a good-time girl. As early as 1929, she was invited to stay at William Randolph Hearst's fabled San Simeon by Marion Davies, not because of her stature in the motion picture industry, but because she was fun. (A glimpse of Carole can be seen in Ken Murray's candid films now shown on the daily tour at San Simeon.)

In the mid-thirties Carole began throwing elaborate parties, often garnering more attention for these doings than for any performance on-screen. Some said there was a particular reason for this flamboyance, including one gushy fan-magazine writer of the day, who noted, "When Carole Lombard

Josephine Hutchinson and Frances Drake at one
of Lombard's parties

A pensive moment in the thirties

finally did return to people and picture work, after Russ Columbo's death, she was a madder, more extravagant 'screwball' than she'd ever been before. It was during this period, in fact, that she gave her famous 'hospital party' which everyone admitted was clever but nobody very much liked. At this affair, if you remember, Carole's guests were met at the door by nurses and internes, and led away to two very amusing 'consultations' with pseudo-doctors. After which they were led to hospital cots and forced to exchange their evening clothes for those horribly unbecoming hospital gowns that open down the back. Food and drinks were served in hospital gadgets, too.

"Well, it was clever. But people said that Carole was certainly going far afield for her laughs these days! People said she certainly must be pretty hard up for something to chuckle about. . . . And people were right!"

Undoubtedly her most famous bash was the one for which she rented the entire amusement park at Venice, California, inviting several hundred Hollywoodites (crew members and electricians as well as stars) to "wear old clothes" and enjoy the rides. Cary Grant, Marlene Dietrich, Henry Fonda, Claudette Colbert, and Randolph Scott were just a few of the many luminaries who attended the party, and had a ball.

Lombard never gave these parties for publicity purposes, but she didn't exactly mind the notoriety either. In the days before she reached stardom, it impressed her name and image not only on the minds of colleagues in the industry, but on fans who followed the coverage of such wingdings in *Photoplay* and other star-gazing magazines.

Some called her irresponsible, while others were not enchanted with her ribald sense of humor. But Carole's generosity, thoughtfulness, and dedication to moviemaking endeared her to every one with whom she worked. On-the-set parties, which were thrown at the completion of every picture, became special events where Carole was concerned; and along with the exchange of gag gifts came personal mementoes that showed great care and planning on her part.

She was so much more than just a romantic madcap.

Lombard's next starring vehicle for Paramount was made under the terms of a new contract engineered by Myron Selznick, her high-powered agent. It paid her $150,000 a picture, with a guarantee of three films and no more. After that she was a free agent.

It made her the highest paid star in Hollywood.

Even in this, she enhanced her screwball image by inserting a clause in the contract with her agent that gave *her* ten percent of *his* earnings! The gag quickly became part of Hollywood lore.

Carole's next film for Paramount doesn't have the modern-day reputation of some other acknowledged "classics," but certainly ranks as one of her all-time best: *The Princess Comes Across*. A curious blend of comedy, murder-mystery, romance, and music, the movie merges all its elements to produce a most satisfying entertainment.

Lombard plays Princess Olga, a Swedish beauty traveling to America on the steamship *Mammoth* with her companion, Lady Gertrude (Alison Skipworth). Her eventual destination is Hollywood, where a contract awaits her to star in the adaptation of *Lavender and Old Lace* called *She Done Him Plenty*. (The name, she adds, will be changed or she'll come back home.) Everyone defers to the lovely princess except brash bandleader

SUPERSTARDOM

King Mantell (Fred MacMurray), who's more interested in her as a woman than as a remote royal figure.

Princess Olga turns out to be Wanda Nash of Brooklyn, pulling a hoax with her canny dramatic coach Gertrude. She's attracted by Mantell and spends some time with him, keeping up the charade until circumstances interfere. Slimy blackmailer Darcy (Porter Hall) is on board, and threatens to expose the "princess." She pays him off, and he then tries to hit up Mantell with a skeleton from *his* closet.

Later that night, Darcy is found murdered in the princess' cabin. She turns to Mantell for help, and he tries to cover up her involvement. It so happens that five international police detectives are on board, traveling to a convention in the U.S.. They volunteer to solve the case, but one of them is murdered when he learns too much; Mantell takes matters into his own hands, both to find the culprit and to save the "princess" from being exposed. Mantell acts as decoy and catches the killer, who turns out to be one of the five "police" experts.

Arriving in New York, Wanda tells Mantell that she cares for him, but she can't afford to ruin the perfect scheme that will bring her Hollywood stardom, everything she's ever longed for. He leaves her, dis-

THE PRINCESS COMES ACROSS (1936). As Princess Olga, also known as Wanda Nash of Brooklyn

appointed in her determination to continue this charade. But when she disembarks and starts to deliver a speech for the radio and press corps, she can't go through with it, and breaks her bogus dialect to confess the truth, so that she can return to the man she loves.

The Princess Comes Across contains one of Lombard's finest and subtlest performances. At the beginning she adopts a standard Swedish accent, and carries herself with Garboesque aloofness, yet she *never* delves into the realm of caricature. The masquerade is funny, but not silly. Asked to name her favorite cinema star, she replies, "Mickey Moose." After maintaining this regal bearing through all the red tape of boarding the ship, and enduring the interference of diffident MacMurray, she finally closes the door of her cabin and says to Skipworth, "I'd like to smack that guy right in the kisser!" It's a hilarious punchline to a masterful shaggy-dog joke, the first time the audience learns her true identity.

Ted Tetzlaff's lighting enhances the Garbo image, with her face held aloft, high cheekbones accentuated, and her head wreathed in flowing scarves. It's a much *softer* image than usual, and mesmerizingly beautiful.

Her byplay with no-nonsense mentor Skipworth is delightful, and the scenes in which she tests her

THE PRINCESS COMES ACROSS (1936).
With Alison Skipworth

THE PRINCESS COMES ACROSS (1936). With Fred MacMurray

princess pose to the limit by venting her anger over being subjected to police investigation are masterfully played. And of course, her final breakdown, when she realizes she just can't go through with the hoax, is exactly what we hope to see in so warm and likeable a character.

The picture remains an oddity, however, for its many-faceted script, reflecting the specialties of the writers who worked on it, from mystery expert Philip MacDonald to comedy pros Don Hartman and Frank Butler. Director William K. Howard fills the picture with the shadows and silhouettes he loved so much, and brings a tense, atmospheric feel to the whodunit aspects of the story. It's not his fault that the murder-mystery has one of the silliest resolutions of the thirties, with red herrings conveniently explained away in one or two lines of absurd banter . . . and it seems unlikely that so skilled a craftsman would have had trouble with the film, as some reports indicate. Lombard's biographer, Larry Swindell, claims that she actually usurped his power during filming and rewrote much of the script, piloting the performances as well with her co-stars and leaving only camera angles for Howard to decide.

Lastly, the film features one of the great kitsch songs of the era, "My Concertina," written by Phil Boutelje and Jack Scholl and sung (quite nicely) by MacMurray, who also "plays" a rendition of "The Flight of the Bumblebee" on his squeeze-box.

The film was another success for Lombard, and also for MacMurray (jointly dubbed "America's Box Office Royalty" by Paramount in trade advertising for the film), who almost didn't make the picture. He was such an "overnight" star that although his name was now above the title, he was still being paid on a starter's contract. Lombard advised him to go on strike and stay away from the studio. Naturally, the young MacMurray was worried about such tactics, but she assured him, "Listen, I know how to handle them. Don't go back until they offer you a lot more money. You're worth it, they know it and sooner or later they'll have to give it to you. Besides, I'll tell them I won't make *The Princess Comes Across* with anyone else." Finally, the studio came across—with more money—and MacMurray again had reason to be grateful for Carole's friendship.

After completing this film, she returned to Universal for the second time within months, this time to make something more than just a fluffy programmer. *My Man Godfrey* (1936), was to become one of the screen's classic comedies, typifying the "screwball" genre of the thirties, cementing (for good) her stardom, and reaffirming her

MY MAN GODFREY (1936). With William Powell

expertise in comic portrayals.

Oddly enough, she was requested for the film by her former husband, William Powell, who was also on loan for the film, from MGM. He knew she'd be right for the part, and after reading the script, she agreed. The film also reunited her with director Gregory La Cava, with whom she'd worked (enjoyably) at Pathé early in her career.

Travis Banton created twenty-four gowns for Carole to wear in *Godfrey*, and Ted Tetzlaff followed up his *Princess* photography with more luminous portraiture. But most importantly, the setting was created for a major comedy characterization, casting Carole as empty-headed rich girl Irene Bullock, who descends upon the city dump in search of a "forgotten man" (a Depression term) to use for a Park Avenue scavenger hunt. So does her sister Cornelia (Gail Patrick), but her snooty manner puts off Godfrey (William Powell), one of the dump's foremost residents, who shoves her onto an ash-pile. Godfrey agrees to go with Irene to the contest, for a five-dollar fee. Irene is delighted, since it's the first time she's ever put one over on her sister.

Irene is so taken with Godfrey that she pulls a coup and, without consulting anyone else, hires him as the family butler and makes him her "protégé." In the Bullock household, where madness reigns, no one ever pays attention to Irene and this is her first attempt to do something concrete.

With a shave and appropriate attire, Godfrey makes a most presentable butler, and it soon becomes clear that he's more than that—a clever, intelligent man who isn't above psychological ploys to set the nutty Bullocks onto a saner path from time to time. Irene is heartbroken, however, because he spurns her amorous advances, determined to succeed in this job and not let romance interfere.

Irene throws a party and one guest, Tommy Gray (Alan Mowbray) recognizes Godfrey as an old schoolmate from Harvard! Godfrey begs him to keep quiet, and the next day they meet for lunch, where Godfrey explains that after leaving his wealthy Boston family and enduring an unsuccessful marriage, he went to pieces, ready to commit suicide, but was dissuaded by the derelicts living by their wits on the banks of the East River. If these people could still look life in the

MY MAN GODFREY (1936). With Gail Patrick, Alice Brady, and William Powell

MY MAN GODFREY (1936). With Eugene Pallette,
Alice Brady, and Mischa Auer

eye, so could he. Now he was hoping to use his success as a butler to
springboard into a more challenging arena.

Godfrey announces that he is
leaving the Bullocks, but not before
making some parting shots.
Blustery Mr. Bullock thinks his for-
tune has dissipated, but Godfrey in-
forms him that he had taken the
liberty of investing money for him,
producing sound dividends and an
impressive portfolio. Fluttery Mrs.
Bullock is upset because *her*
protégé, a sponger called Carlo, has
to endure such family turmoil, but a
new and strong Mr. Bullock finally

summons the determination to kick
Carlo out of the house. And snide
Cornelia is taught a lesson when
Godfrey explains that he never sank
to her level by revealing that she
had hidden some jewels she accused
him of stealing.

Godfrey leaves the Bullocks to
pursue his own dream: building a
nightclub at the city dump and putting all the "forgotten men" to
work. Opening night is a huge success, and Irene comes to visit Godfrey in his office. Having proved
himself, he no longer has to im-
pose barriers between himself and
his former "boss," but it still takes

Lombard in the mid-thirties

persuasion on her part to get him to stand still and say yes, when she drags the Mayor into the office to marry them.

My Man Godfrey is one of the quintessential thirties comedies, with many elements that came to define the screwball genre, principally the masquerade of someone rich as someone poor, and the empty-headedness of the monied classes. Mrs. Bullock is played by Alice Brady, who alternated in such roles with Billie Burke. A scatter-brained woman immersed in her own world, when her daughter Irene goes on a hunger strike and asks mournfully, "What is food?" she answers brightly, "Something you eat!"

Her "protégé" Carlo, beautifully played by Mischa Auer, is a self-proclaimed artistic genuis. When Irene is feeling low, Mrs. Bullock prevails upon Carlo to cheer her up by doing his gorilla imitation. He balks but she insists, so he agrees, muttering, "I'll do it, but my heart won't be in it." He then proceeds to hunch over, distort his face, and leap around the room, leaving Irene more bewildered than amused.

Presiding over this menagerie is wealthy Mr. Bullock, who hasn't a clue to his family's antic behavior and has given up trying. He is por-trayed by gravel-voiced Eugene Pallette in another definitive characterization. Other perfor-mances by Gail Patrick, Alan Mowbray, Jean Dixon, Franklin Pangborn, and Grady Sutton add to the comic atmosphere.

Carole plays the dizziest dame of her career in *Godfrey*, incapable of formulating one intelligent thought and propelled only by a competitive spirit to outdo her flamboyant mother and snooty sister. Unable to get a tumble from Powell, she final-ly tries fainting, and he carries her up to her bedroom; but when he realizes that she's faking, he decides to revive her by dumping her into a cold shower. Instead of being angry, the sopping-wet Lombard runs from the bathroom shouting happily, "Godfrey loves me!"

Hers is a most challenging characterization to put across, because there is no basis in reality. She earned an appropriate compli-ment for her work from *Variety*, which reported, "Miss Lombard's role is the more difficult of the two, since it calls for pressure acting all the way, and it was no simple trick to refrain from overworking the in-sanity plea in a many-sided assign-ment. It's Powell's job to be normal and breezily comic in the madcap household, and that doesn't require stretching for him."

Carole's work also won her the ultimate Hollywood compliment: nomination for an Academy Award as Best Actress of the Year. Unfor-tunately, her competition was stiff (Irene Dunne in *Theodora Goes Wild*, Gladys George in *Valiant is*

SWING HIGH, SWING LOW (1937). With Fred MacMurray

the Word for Carrie, Norma Shearer in *Romeo and Juliet*, and Luise Rainer in *The Great Ziegfeld*), and she lost out to Miss Rainer. Still, it was a great honor and the ultimate victory for an actress who had been ignored so long.

Another recognition came from co-workers on the film, as described in a publicity story released by Universal: "Carole Lombard, regarded as a glamourous star by the millions who see her on the screen, is just a 'good guy' to those who worked on the *My Man Godfrey* sets.

"The cameramen, sound technicians, the electricians and prop boys all say, 'She's tops.' When the picture was finished they

presented her with an enormous china egg, autographed and decorated until it looked like the egg that hatched the golden goose. The inscription on it read, 'To Carole, a Good Egg.' "

William Powell, Mischa Auer, and Alice Brady also copped Oscar nominations; scenarists Eric Hatch and Morrie Ryskind won their share of praise, while the film earned director Gregory La Cava, a well-deserved Academy nomination. La Cava, an inventive filmmaker who liked a party atmosphere on his sets, never settled into the Hollywood groove, and enjoyed a spotty career of which *Godfrey* was a definite high-point.

Carole returned to Paramount to

SWING HIGH, SWING LOW (1937). With Fred MacMurray

star in one of her most ambitious vehicles, *Swing High, Swing Low*. Based on the stage play *Burlesque*, which had been filmed in 1929 as *The Dance of Life* (with Nancy Carroll and Hal Skelly) the story was rejuvenated by Virginia Van Upp and Oscar Hammerstein, with Mitchell Leisen directing. Paramount paired Lombard with Fred MacMurray for the third time in what promised to be one of the studio's major releases of 1937.

The film opens as the co-stars meet in "cute" thirties fashion: Maggie King is leaning on the railing of a ship passing through the Panama Canal, and Skid Johnson is on sentry duty ashore, calling out wisecracks to the blonde beauty. They make a date for that night. He learns that she's an unemployed entertainer trying to earn her living as a hairdresser on this ship; and she finds that he's in the Army for want of something better to do. He's about to be discharged, and mentions that he might go back to trumpet-playing. When she scoffs, he picks up a horn from one of the band members in a nightclub and gives her an impressive sampling of his talent. While he's playing, she's accosted by a hot-blooded Panamanian (Anthony Quinn) and a brawl erupts. Skid is arrested, and in an effort to bail him out and explain the situation to a judge, Maggie misses her boat and is forced to remain in Panama.

She moves in with Skid and his songwriting pal Harry (Charles Butterworth) and immediately encourages Skid to get a job playing trumpet. He's irresponsible, and Maggie is warned, "you're leading with your chin falling for a guy like Skid," but she believes in him, and wangles a job from nightclub owner Murphy (Cecil Cunningham) for both of them. She works as a dancer, and he plays in the band.

Soon Skid steps out on his own, as soloist, and Maggie does a romantic number with him, "I Hear a Call to Arms." They're a success, and soon they are married, although Skid's footloose nature remains a constant threat. So does voluptuous vocalist Anita Alvarez (Dorothy Lamour), who has not-so-secret designs on him.

When Skid gets an offer to go to New York, he doesn't want to leave Maggie behind, but she insists, and he promises to send for her as soon as he's got some money. Success goes to his head, however, and he abandons Maggie, spending most of his time with the alluring Anita. Finally, Maggie goes to New York to see her husband; when she can't even arrange a meeting, she leaves him a note announcing her intention to get a divorce. She meets handsome Harvey Dexter (Harvey Stephens) and plans to marry him.

Skid learns the news and comes to visit his wife and her new fiancé. He pretends not to care, but his

Posing in a swim suit in 1936

behavior is frantic and ultimately sad. After Maggie leaves him, he lets his career slide, and becomes the biggest has-been in New York. Drinking dissipates his health, and when in desperation he tries to return to the Army, he finds that even they won't have him any more.

His last chance is a radio come-back arranged by his friend Harry. Skid is too weak to perform, but Maggie is persuaded to come to the broadcast and cheer him on. With her help, he manages to revive his spirits and give some indication of the old Skid Johnson talent. The message is clear: they belong together.

The *Burlesque* plot is the stuff of which clichés and parodies are made, and unfortunately, *Swing High, Swing Low* cannot steer completely clear of these pitfalls. But Leisen's direction (coupled with Tetzlaff's camerawork) is so sensitive and the lead performances so strong that the film does create some effective moments.

Although famed vocal coach Al Siegel worked with Lombard prior to shooting, she remains completely fresh and unpretentious in her delivery of the film's key songs. "I Hear a Call to Arms" is a mood piece, sold as much by its unique presentation as by her vocalizing: Lombard cuddles into MacMurray's arms and sings while he plays obligato. The first time she sings "If It Isn't Pain, Then It Isn't Love," it's an informal tryout with the band, and she grimaces at her own work, admitting afterward that it wasn't very good. (Said Leisen, "I insisted that Carole do her own singing. She didn't think she could do it and she begged me to have somebody dub her numbers, but I said that nobody could have the same quality of voice and it would be unbelievable. So she did it and it came out beautifully.")

Lombard is exquisite in *Swing High, Swing Low*, and her conviction in dramatic scenes with MacMurray makes us want to believe the outlandish storyline, but that's a tall assignment. Skid's irresponsibility is just a bit *too* much. His meteoric rise in New York is conveyed through a typical "success" montage, while his fall is delineated by an amazingly precipitous "skid." The eloquent summation of his condition is spoken by an Army doctor who tells him solemnly, "You're all shot."

Critical reception to *Swing High, Swing Low* was mixed. Frank S. Nugent in *The New York Times* commended Lombard and MacMurray for "raising a routine story to a routine-plus picture," and felt that "*Swing High, Swing Low*, like most Ferris wheels, doesn't go anywhere—at least, nowhere that you have not been. Its players are worthy of better treatment."

NOTHING SACRED (1937). With Charles Winninger and Fredric March

On the other hand, fan-oriented *Photoplay* exulted, "That vivid climb toward stardom started by Carole Lombard in *20th Century* three years ago here reaches glory, for, while this photoplay is the smoothest possible blend of laughter and tears, or torch numbers, fine production, direction and camera work, it is Lombard's art that makes this a great emotional experience."

Moviegoers reacted more in line with *Photoplay*'s assessment than the *Times*', and *Swing High, Swing Low* became Paramount's biggest money-maker of the year. The studio's large fee for Carole was happily justified. (Incidentally, the film was remade eleven years later by 20th Century-Fox as *When My Baby Smiles at Me*, with Dan Dailey and Betty Grable. Because of this remake, the original is sadly kept off television and out of circulation). Advertising stressed such angles as "Carole sings for the first time," and proclaimed, "Romance! The most powerful love story either Carole or Fred has ever starred in. An up and down romance as real as young love itself."

Another ad-line promised "Excitement! Fred in another of those brawls that had you cheering in *The Trail of the Lonesome Pine*." Interestingly, Fred's brawling partner in that scene was young Anthony Quinn, making one of his earliest screen appearances.

NOTHING SACRED (1937). With Charles Winninger

He had been on the Paramount lot doing a small role in Cecil B. DeMille's *The Plainsman* and had attracted no little attention when he told the director where to get off. Lombard spotted him one day and promised him a part in her next picture.

Quinn recalled in his autobiography, "The picture was called *Swing High, Swing Low*. Carole Lombard had kept her word and I reported on the set to work with her. I guess I had a slight crush on her. She was so sophisticated and frank, so honest, you couldn't be a phony with her. But I didn't know what to talk to her about. I thought movie stars must all be terribly cultured, incredibly wise. When I suddenly found myself near this goddess, I felt lost.

"In three days I finished my scene with her. Everybody seemed to be happy with my work. Carole had complimented me several times and occasionally, when she thought I could do better, she would say to Mitch Leisen, 'Let's do it again.' She was protecting me. Every night she'd invite me in for a drink, and she kept saying, 'You're going to have a big career, kid.' "*

Carole became Quinn's mentor at Paramount, taking him under her wing as she had done so many others, introducing him to the right people and counseling him on financial matters. Needless to add, her prediction of big things for Quinn was right on target.

* Anthony Quinn, *The Original Sin*, Little, Brown and Co., Boston, 1972, p. 236.

NOTHING SACRED (1937). With Fredric March and Walter Connolly

Bigger things still were happening in Carole's career.

Anticipating the end of her three-picture deal with Paramount, Lombard's agent inked an even *more* lucrative deal with his producer-brother, David O. Selznick. With one film still due her home studio, Carole went into production for Selznick's memorable comedy, *Nothing Sacred* (1937).

Along with *My Man Godfrey*, *Nothing Sacred* tops the list of Carole's classic "screwball" comedies. This one has the distinction of a Ben Hecht script, and the additional treat of seeing Carole in Technicolor. Larry Swindell has written perceptively, "Mistaken as a great film almost immediately, it was never that. But it was a great screenplay, and one of Hollywood's rare examples of satire achieved within a farce structure."

In the story, New York *Morning Star* reporter Wally Cook (Fredric March) tries to make up for a story that backfired on his publisher, Stone (Walter Connolly), by following through a human interest lead about a girl in Warsaw, Vermont who is apparently dying of radium poisoning and only has six months to live. Stone lets him try his luck.

Cook travels to the sleepy Vermont town and finds its natives openly hostile to (a) New Yorkers and (b) reporters. Being both, he is greeted appropriately, and as he walks by one home, a little boy runs out to the sidewalk and bites him on the leg! Finally he locates the girl in question, Hazel Flagg (Lombard). Unbeknownst to him, she's just been told by her friend, Dr. Downer (Charles Winninger) that his initial diagnosis was wrong and she's in perfect health. Hazel is not happy about the news. First, she's been planning to blow her savings on a trip to New York City, and second, "It's kind of startling to be brought to life twice, and both times in Warsaw."

Enter Wally Cook. He tells Hazel that the *Morning Star* wants to bring her to New York, and make her last months the happiest she's ever had. Hazel is ecstatic, and her momentary doubts about deceiving the reporter are wiped away by the thought of seeing New York; she even arranges to take Dr. Downer along.

In New York, Hazel quickly becomes the city's sweetheart—all appropriately reported on the front page of the *Star*. She's wined and dined, feted and fussed over. What's more, she and Wally fall in love. But he can't bear to think of her dying, and she can't bear to tell him the truth.

Finally, the truth *does* come out, when a Viennese specialist is called in and pronounces her fit as a fiddle. Both Cook and publisher Stone are stymied, until an embarrassed Hazel says she wishes she could go away and face the end alone, "like an elephant." The next morning, Hazel disappears (along with Wally) and leaves behind a farewell letter to the people of New York, saying she's gone off to face the end alone—like an elephant. Her memory untarnished, the newspaper's credibility undimmed, she and Wally sail off together on their honeymoon.

Nothing Sacred is not the powerhouse film Ben Hecht's cynical script would suggest, but it *is* great fun. His description of New York—"where the slickers and know-it-alls sell gold bricks to each other"—sets the tone for the rest of the film.

Carole is sublime as the innocent girl who just can't bear to give up a trip to New York. She's somewhat remorseful, but with a few drinks in her (as in one nightclub scene), she gets misty-eyed listening to M.C. Frank Fay tell her own (bogus) story!

At one point, feeling especially guilty, she decides to get out of her dilemma by faking a suicide, jumping off a dock into the Hudson River. March finds out about it and tries to stop her, but inadvertently shoves her over the ledge instead! After fishing her out, they sit together in a packing crate on the pier. The view of Lombard huddling with March, wearing his jacket and smiling through the strands of hair streaming down her forehead, is unforgettable.

But undoubtedly the movie's most famous scene comes when March, having learned the truth

TRUE CONFESSION (1937). With Fred MacMurray

about Carole, does his best to make her appear ill for publisher Walter Connolly, who's coming to check up on her. He boxes her around, to make her work up some sweat, and then apologizes before pulling the coup de grace: a sock on the chin that knocks her cold. It's all for naught, however, since Connolly has witnessed the whole charade. Learning this, Lombard strikes back by popping March in the face; now *he's* out flat . . . and of course she's immediately sorry she did it.

A sequence of pictures showing March socking Lombard comprised the most-used advertising campaign of the film, often accompanied by tags like "the fight of the century." But the sequence always ended with a shot of March bending over the unconscious Carole and kissing her, lest potential moviegoers think wrongly of the comedy film. The sequence also garnered maximum publicity coverage in scores of newspapers and magazines.

Nothing Sacred was held over for three weeks at New York's Radio City Music Hall, and won Carole a new collection of personal rave reviews, even from critics who were less than enchanted with the film. *Life* magazine said it was "acted with finesse by an unbeatable pair of light comedy experts, Carole Lombard and Fredric March." *The New York Times* called it "one of the merrier jests of the cinema

year" and praised the "agreeable trouping of a perfect passel of clowns."

Lombard immediately moved back to Paramount to complete her three-picture contract there, with *True Confession*. Interestingly enough, it was released at the same time as *Nothing Sacred*, in time for the winter holidays in 1937.

True Confession again spotlighted Carole the Comedienne but gave her a most unenviable assignment: playing a completely stupid character, a basically sweet girl who is a compulsive liar. It was difficult enough to pull off the addlebrained characterization in *My Man Godfrey*, but this one proved too big a job even for lovable Lombard.

Briefly, the story pits soft-headed, soft-hearted Helen Bartlett against her true-blue husband (Fred MacMurray), a starving lawyer who insists on honesty and integrity. Carole secretly goes job-hunting to supplement their income, and is interviewed by a lecherous "employer" at his home. When he chases her, she makes a fast exit, leaving her pocketbook behind. Going to fetch it later, she finds the man dead, and the police on their way to investigate. Flustered by the grilling she gets from Inspector Darsey (Edgar Kennedy), she actually admits to the murder, thinking that this will give her husband a prominent court case.

TRUE CONFESSION (1937). With Fred MacMurray

Husband Kenneth makes a heartfelt plea to the jury that the killing was justifiable homicide, and miraculously, Helen is freed. The notoriety of the case makes her husband a success, and brings her lucrative offers to write her life story. When Kenneth learns that it's all been another lie, he walks out on Helen, and she again tries deception to bring him back. He isn't fooled, but he can't help loving her.

There is no charm to *True Confession*. Director Wesley Ruggles, increasingly heavy-handed as the years passed, allowed scenes and situations to drag and become protracted, spoiling their comic potential. And the incidental role of John Barrymore only adds to the oddity of this film. Introduced as a lovable eccentric, he is then revealed to be a crazy extortionist, and a possible murderer. His fate is left unresolved as MacMurray tells him off, and. he just walks out of the film!

The basic problem is the total unbelievability of the premise and the main characters. Even Lombard's considerable charm can't overcome those obstacles.

Still, *True Confession* was well

received when it hit theaters in late 1937. At this time, Carole could do no wrong. She used her final Paramount vehicle to pay back a great debt to John Barrymore, now down on his luck and reduced to making B-pictures. She not only got him the part in *Confession*, but insisted on giving him star billing above the title along with herself and MacMurray.

But she—and a great many others—were in for a shock regarding her next film. *Fools for Scandal* (1938) was Lombard's only venture for Warner Brothers. The studio rolled out the red carpet, and presented her with its latest imported leading man (Fernand Gravet) and a proven director, Mervyn LeRoy. But the resulting film was an unqualified disaster.

She plays the part of Kay Winters, a Hollywood movie star on vacation in Paris. There she catches the eye of worldly but penniless Gravet, who makes it his ambition in life to woo and win her. He follows her to London and contrives to get himself hired as her new chef, without her knowledge. His presence in her home becomes the talk of the town, and the bane of suitor Ralph Bellamy's existence

FOOLS FOR SCANDAL (1938). With Fernand Gravet

FOOLS FOR SCANDAL (1938). With Ralph Bellamy

. . . until Kay relents and finally admits that she's in love with him.

There's hardly a good word to say about this film. Lombard looks exquisite (photographed again by Ted Tetzlaff) and wears some beautiful clothes (by Travis Banton), but in the first fifteen minutes of the film, she is seen in a most unbecoming brunette wig.

The characterizations are strictly cardboard, with no attempt to create a basis of believability so that we *care* about the people on-screen. Even a talk-song by Rodgers and Hart, "Fools for Scandal," is silly and superfluous.

This film isn't just feather-weight . . . it's feather-*brained*.

Although columnist Walter Winchell called it "a Lombardment of Laughs" (just right for advertising copy), most of the legitimate reviewers had other things to say: "pretty dull stuff" (*Variety*) . . . "ponderous" (*The New York Times*).

It was Carole Lombard's most conspicuous flop, after riding the crest of the wave as a successful comedienne. And in the wake of this failure, she stayed off-screen for nearly a year, tending to more personally important matters.

By now the story is a Hollywood legend.

Four years after co-starring in a picture, Gable and Lombard met again, and this time fell in love.

Apparently *he* went after *her*, but when their steady dates turned into a lasting affair, *she* began to prod *him* about some eventual outcome to their partnership. There was one major stumbling-block: Gable was still legally married to Rhea Langham, and Mrs. Gable was not about to give up her successful husband without a struggle . . . more monetary in nature than personal.

Gable was reluctant to cough up the half-million dollars Rhea demanded, so he and Lombard became Hollywood's most famous unmarried couple.

Fan magazines then were a far cry from the journals which fill today's newsstands. Scandal was not their bread-and-butter in the thirties, and there was no attempt to exploit the Gable-Lombard situation; in fact, constant coverage of the story resulted in widespread public empathy, with fans waiting for legal hurdles to be cleared so this "perfect couple" could be wed.

In the meantime, they commanded prime attention, firstly because Gable was movies' number-one box-office star (named "The King" in 1937 by columnist Ed Sullivan), and secondly, because Lombard provided such good copy. She and Clark never tired of devis-

LOMBARD AND GABLE

ing gag gifts for each other, and news of these presents (ranging from a gift-wrapped jalopy to a ham with Gable's picture pasted on) was devoured by movie fans everywhere.

During their three years of companionship, Gable and Lombard learned much about each other. Lombard did not hesitate to make her most private discovery known in Hollywood circles, admitting that Clark was a "lousy" lover, but between themselves, they learned of many personality contrasts. Gable was stingy, Lombard was generous. Carole lived for fun, but Clark took himself more seriously. She enjoyed making movies, but to him it was just a job.

Carole decided that she really loved him, though, and that she would adapt herself to him in every way she could. Since his principal pastime was hunting, she determined to make herself as good an outdoorsman as he, and like it. In 1939, Faith Baldwin wrote, "She can handle a shotgun as easily as a lipstick. She can pile out of bed at five in the morning, yank on boots, wool riding pants, a lumber jacket—not the most becoming of costumes—drink some scalding coffee and start out in a station wagon for a duck blind, over a mile of bumpy road into some God-

With Gable at a rehearsal for Lux Radio Theatre in 1937

forsaken wilderness where she'll kneel in mud and water, waiting and motionless, until the wedge-shaped flight of birds passes overhead against the morning sky. And when it's time to eat, it won't be crepes suzette!"*

Gable wasn't exactly a women's lib advocate. As his reporter friend Adela Rogers St. Johns later wrote, "A woman would *try*, he said, but no woman was ever happy in marriage unless the man was the head of the family."

After nearly three years, Gable's divorce came through, and the couple were married quietly in Kingman, Arizona on March 29,

1939. Few Hollywood marriages ever rivalled theirs for national attention. They moved into their new home, a ranch in Encino, that summer, and at year's end, Carole proudly stood beside her husband at the Atlanta premiere of his starring film, *Gone With the Wind*.

Carole talked seriously about retiring from movies—as Gable did, from time to time. Her principal goal was to raise a family. David Niven recalls visiting them in September, 1939, before he left to join the war in England.

"They were so happy and evidently had so much together that I wondered aloud if there could be anything else they had their eyes on. Carole looked up into Clark's face.

* *Photoplay*, May, 1939, pp. 18-19.

116

With Clark Gable at a preview of his latest film, several months before their marriage

The day after their marriage in March, 1939

"I'll tell you what Pappy wants,' she said quietly, 'and I just hope to Christ I can give it to him . . . He wants a kid.'

"Yeah, that's right,' said Clark, stroking her hair. 'I'd give my right arm for a son.'

"There was a semi-embarrassed silence till Carole let out one of her famous yelps of laughter. 'And he's sure as hell working on it!'"*

The Gables never had a child; sadly, Carole could not conceive. But she gave Gable everything else a man could want.

Most of all, she made him laugh. After her death, Gable recalled for Adela Rogers St. Johns, "One day we were looking around at our ranch here in the San Fernando Valley and it was beautiful—one of those California days. We were just—lazy—strolling around—gabbing and I said, 'Mother, we're awfully lucky, you and I—all this and each other—anything you want we haven't got?' You know what she said, standing there looking lovely as a dream? She said, 'Well, I could do with another load of manure for the south forty.' " **

* David Niven, *Bring On the Empty Horses*, G.P. Putnam's, New York, 1975, p. 43.

** Adela Rogers St. Johns, *The Honeycomb*, Doubleday, New York, 1969, pp. 181-182.

Carole returned to films in 1939 with a new outlook on her career. Having proven herself in comedy—and made some of the best screen comedies ever—she wanted to establish herself as a dramatic actress as well. Those who understood the artistry of her performances never doubted her acting ability, but Hollywood in general and the public at large had her typecast as a comedienne.

Her first venture into the dramatic was a simple domestic story called *Made for Each Other*, produced by David Selznick and directed by John Cromwell. Her co-star was James Stewart.

He portrays John Mason, a young lawyer working in the office of gruff Judge Doolittle (Charles Coburn) and living at home with his mother (Lucile Watson). During a business trip to Boston, he meets and marries Jane (Lombard), but their marriage seems to be jinxed from the start. Receiving the news, his overprotective mother faints, and makes no secret of her feelings. His boss says matter-of-factly, "Last year there were nearly half a million divorces in this country. Congratulations, Mason."

The couple is denied a honeymoon by Doolittle's refusal to reschedule a case, and financial worries demand that John's mother live with them. Whenever Mrs. Mason starts her "subtle" needling, Jane repeats under her breath, "I

THE NEW LOMBARD

won't say anything . . . I won't say anything."

But things get worse instead of better. With the arrival of a baby, the financial problem grows more acute, and John simply hasn't got the guts to ask the Judge for a raise. Even the promotion he's counting on goes to someone else—with Doolittle coldly announcing the decision during a dinner party given for him by John and Jane.

Pressures mount to the extent that on New Year's Eve, in the midst of a supposed celebration, they decide to separate. But before the evening passes, they are brought together—by the tragic illness of their baby, who has contracted a rare and serious disease. There is no serum available in New York; the only specimen is in a hospital in Salt Lake City. John frantically enlists Judge Doolittle's help, and he volunteers five thousand dollars to pay a breakneck flyer who agrees to brave a blizzard and attempt to reach New York with the serum.

The ordeal brings out the humanity in Mrs. Mason, as well as the Judge, and when the baby is saved, a new light seems to shine on the marriage of John and Jane Mason.

Time magazine said that "this mundane, domestic chronicle has more impact than all the hurricanes, sandstorms and earth-

MADE FOR EACH OTHER (1939). With James Stewart

quakes manufactured in Hollywood last season," and *Newsweek* called Carole's "the best performance of her career."

Producer Selznick heralded the film with an announcement ad proclaiming "CAROLE CRIES! It's a David O. Selznick stroke of showmanship to make Lombard go dramatic!"

Made for Each Other is no masterpiece, using sure-fire heart-tug devices to manipulate its audience's emotions, but the material is so well handled that one can hardly complain. Lombard and Stewart bring such conviction to their roles that they tower above the script and make of it something very special.

Carole thought highly of the film, and was pleased to return to movies with such a well-received effort. Her only gripe was the cliffhanger climax, which wasn't in the original script. It came about when the producer's brother (and Carole's agent) Myron Selznick fell ill in Los Angeles and required a special serum found only in New York. David chartered a plane to fly in the valuable medicine, watching the clock anxiously, since every hour counted. The plane completed the flight in record time, and his brother's life was saved. When the crisis passed, Selznick declared, "This is too good to waste on Myron . . . let's put it in the picture." And they did.

MADE FOR EACH OTHER (1939). With Lucile Watson

Carole enjoyed working with director John Cromwell, and joined forces with him once more in 1939, this time at RKO, where she signed a four-picture contract. This new film was, like *Made for Each Other*, in a dramatic vein, and again, Carole carried it off beautifully. The title: *In Name Only*.

Carole plays Julie Eden, an attractive young widow who's living with her daughter and divorced sister in Connecticut for the summer. She chances to meet handsome Alec Walker (Cary Grant), and he wants to see more of her. She brushes him off when she learns that he's married, but he explains that the marriage is a sham;

his wife Maida (Kay Francis) simply will not give him the satisfaction of a divorce. She married him for prestige and money, and she's not about to give it up. Yet Maida has Alec's parents, and all of their friends, fooled into thinking she's the "victim" and he's the heartless philanderer.

Julie moves to New York rather than endure the heartache of Alec's love, and he follows her after Maida finally agrees to obtain a divorce in Paris. They're reunited, and deliriously happy, until Maida returns and reveals that she was fooling.

It seems hopeless, and Alec goes on a drinking binge, winding up in a hotel room where he opens a win-

IN NAME ONLY (1939). With Cary Grant and Peggy Ann Garner

*IN NAME ONLY (1939). With Charles Coburn, Nella
Walker, Kay Francis, and Cary Grant*

dow and foolishly falls asleep sitting in front of it. Next morning,
he's got pneumonia; Julie comes to
care for him, but when she calls his
family doctor, he takes Alec to a
hospital and refuses to allow Julie
to see him.

She is finally admitted to his
room when the doctor realizes that
she's the only one Alec really wants
to see. Julie tells him that
everything is set, and they will be
married, holding back her tears as
she knows this can never happen.

As she's leaving the anteroom of
his hospital suite, Maida enters,
and unaware of the circumstances,
scorns Julie and haughtily brags
that she's got Alec for good, that
she married him for his money and
will not let him go. She doesn't

realize that Alec's parents have just
stepped into the room and
overheard her faux pas. At last,
everything crystallizes, and Julie is
accepted, while Maida is left standing outside . . . alone.

In Name Only is easily
pigeonholed as "soap opera," yet it
escapes whatever negative con-
notations that phrase may have for
some. In every way it's an excellent
picture.

First, the setting is real. So much
of the film's first half takes place
outdoors that it would have been
ludicrous to follow studio policy
and shoot on make-believe sets.
Director Cromwell took his cast
outdoors to create a believable setting.

Second, the performances are

vividly real. Carole is subdued throughout the film, making her very few emotional outbursts doubly effective. She's beautiful, of course, but not glamorized; near the end of the film, when her character is haggard and distraught over Grant's illness, she *looks* the part. Cary Grant matches her all the way, delivering one of his most thoughtful dramatic performances.

Only Kay Francis' role smacks of old-fashioned hokum, but this is easily forgivable in light of the picture's many virtues. Although she is set up as an obvious target, her comeuppance is handled with restraint. After she's blundered her way out of the family's good graces, Grant's parents and Lombard walk into his sick-room, leaving her behind. The camera then sees Francis from inside the room as the door slowly closes on her, standing alone and speechless. (*Motion Picture Herald* reported, "By (this) time ... the preview audience was affected to the point of booing her just as in the old days.")

The New York Times wrote, "Miss Lombard plays her poignant role with all the fragile intensity and contained passion that have lifted her to dramatic eminence," calling the film "one of the most adult and enjoyable pictures of the season." Other critics agreed, and *In Name Only* was held over for three weeks at Radio City Music Hall, although like its predecessor,

it was not the long-range smash hit Carole could have used.

Her two-time director, John Cromwell, remembers her as "just a joy, a wonderful, wonderful gal. She was enough of an actress to display her personality and her great charm, but I don't think she did any more than just to fill the ordinary aspirations of somebody in that position. I think she was interested in other things in life besides being an actress." Cromwell's comment reflects Carole's preoccupation with her new husband at the time she made both *Made for Each Other* and *In Name Only*.

While *In Name Only* was playing at Radio City, RKO announced its forthcoming product for the trade and highlighted Carole's next, declaring, "No waits between big ones ... this one shooting right now." Three weeks later RKO had to apologize to theater-owners for a delay due to Lombard's illness—an emergency appendectomy—but upon her recovery, shooting resumed on *Vigil in the Night*, bringing her together with the studio's leading director, George Stevens.

Carole claimed that she didn't care if a role were comic or dramatic, so long as it was good. But *Vigil in the Night* (1940) was an obvious attempt to seize a ripe, dramatic role and play it for all it was worth.

Not that *Vigil* is a bravura kind of film; just the opposite. Lombard

IN NAME ONLY (1939). With Cary Grant

plays Anne Lee, a dedicated nurse in England who takes the blame when her sister Lucy (Anne Shirley) allows a child to die one night through neglect. Anne moves to another hospital and meets devoted Dr. Prescott (Brian Aherne), who falls in love with her but realizes that nursing is her whole life. Anne is fired when she refused to play ball with lecherous hospital benefactor Bowley (Julien Mitchell), but she is called back to service when a plague strikes the community. Manning the deadly isolation ward is a near-suicidal task, but Anne volunteers, and her unselfishness inspires others to follow suit, including her sister Lucy, who is anxious to make up for her earlier neglect . . . and who dies after serving bravely and saving a young boy's life. After the plague passes, Bowley, whose son was claimed by the disease, rewards Prescott's dedication by supporting

Lombard
around 1940

VIGIL IN THE NIGHT (1940). With Anne Shirley

a new, badly needed facility, and seeing Anne reinstated as his colleague.

Vigil in the Night is a moving film with melodramatic touches that weaken—but don't destroy—its overall effectiveness. Lombard's performance is superb, with excellent support from Aherne, Anne Shirley, Robert Coote, Ethel Griffies, and Julien Mitchell.

Director Stevens and cameraman Robert De Grasse conceived some powerful hospital sequences, including a climactic scene in which Shirley works all night to save a boy's life—quiet, alone, silhouetted against the darkened room—that's so visually eloquent it remains in one's memory long after the film is over.

RKO called the film "A.J. Cronin's greatest story since *The Citadel*," and George Stevens' audience-appeal attitude toward the script—with its clearly drawn villains and melodramatic touches, not to mention a happy ending—should have made it a great success. Critical reaction was divided, but audiences weren't: they stayed away en masse. It was considered too heavy, and salesmanship foundered against the negative word-of-mouth.

To this day *Vigil in the Night* is underrated—or more to the point, ignored. It doesn't deserve such obscurity: for Stevens' thoughtful direction, and for Lombard's fine performance, it should be seen.

The same may be said for her next dramatic film, *They Knew What They Wanted*, directed by Garson Kanin from the play by Sidney Howard, and co-starring Charles Laughton.

Laughton plays Tony, an illiterate Italian-American grape farmer who comes to San Francisco on business, and falls in love with a waitress in a short-order restaurant. Too bashful to say anything to her, he waits until he gets home and then has his foreman

Joe (William Gargan) compose a respectful love letter to her. The letter paints a rose-colored picture of Tony and his station in life, and waitress Amy (Lombard), who dreams of escaping her humdrum life, answers in kind—having *her* friend type the response in proper business form! Their correspondence leads to a marriage proposal, and Amy takes the train to the Napa Valley to meet her prospective husband for the first time.

Tony asks Joe to meet her at the station, making the shock of en-

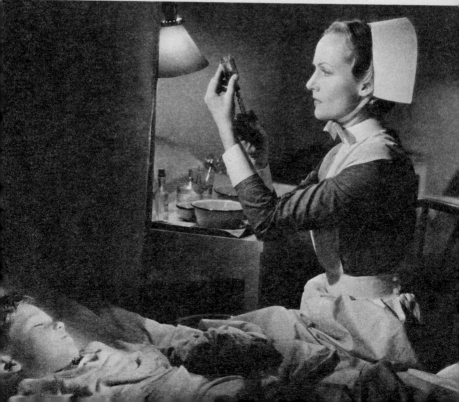

VIGIL IN THE NIGHT (1940). As Anne Lee

THEY KNEW WHAT THEY WANTED (1940).
With Charles Laughton

countering her mail-order husband doubly severe, for it's *Joe*'s picture Tony has sent as his own. Tony is sweet and good-natured, but hardly attractive, and not what the letters have made him out to be. Amy sadly resigns herself to her fate, and there is a wedding celebration. Tony drinks too much, and in the excitement falls from the roof of his house, breaking both legs.

Amy is a kind and devoted nurse, and during Tony's recuperation she grows to appreciate his affection and kindness. But she is also tempted by the sullen magnetism of Joe, and one night, he seduces her.

She feels she has betrayed Tony, and finally builds up the courage to tell him that she is pregnant. Tony wants to kill Joe, but has no anger for Amy, offering to raise the child as his own. She cannot live with that, however, and goes away to have her baby, hoping to return some day to the man who cares more about her than any other.

Sidney Howard's play tells a beautiful story; it's a shame that censorship diluted that story every time the play was filmed (in 1928, as *The Secret Hour*, with Pola Negri and Jean Hersholt, and in 1930, as *A Lady to Love*, with Vilma Banky and Edward G. Robinson). Abrupt editing and muddled narrative also undermine this 1940 version, but there is so much at the foundation that *They Knew What They Wanted* retains considerable emotional impact. Alfred Newman's beautiful music score is a great asset, as was his work on *Vigil in the Night*.

Lombard is wonderful as Amy, the dreamy-eyed waitress who longs for an opportunity to hop off the treadmill and enjoy life. She doesn't need dialogue to convey her emotions; they flash across the screen through her marvelously expressive face and voice.

Unfortunately, the story development is weak. Her growing attachment to Tony is abrupt and unrealized; at one point she tells him that he's "the swellest guy in the world," but we haven't seen the evolution of this feeling. Likewise, her love/hate relationship with William Gargan is just too sudden and sure; from the moment she arrives, there are furtive glances as portents of things to come.

In truth, *They Knew What They Wanted* is Laughton's film. As the

THEY KNEW WHAT THEY WANTED (1940). With William Gargan and Harry Carey

THEY KNEW WHAT THEY WANTED (1940).
With Charles Laughton

simple-minded Italian, he's amazingly good, somehow escaping the pitfall of turning the character into a second-string Henry Armetta. The supporting cast includes Harry Carey as a wise country doctor, Frank Fay as a sanctimonious priest, and two young movie newcomers, Karl Malden and Tom Ewell, in small but noticeable roles.

Director Garson Kanin's book *Hollywood* includes some interesting observations on Carole's attitude toward work. She showed no temperament, was always on time, always on cue, and always knew her lines to perfection. She attended filming even on days when she had no scenes to shoot.

"She wanted to be around," Kanin explains, "to stay with the feel of things. She did not want to lose the momentum of work. On these days, she would hang around the set, watching; come along and look at the rushes; talk to various members of the cast. She was valuable.

"I thought her a fine actress, one of the finest I had ever encountered ... If Carole did six takes they were six *different* takes. Each one had some small development, some sense of growth. A nuance that had not appeared before. There was always something going on inside of Carole."*

* Garson Kanin, *Hollywood*, Viking Press, New York, 1974, p. 59.

On the set of THEY KNEW WHAT THEY WANTED with director Garson Kanin and Clark Gable

MR. AND MRS. SMITH (1941). With Robert Montgomery

One of the things that occupied Carole's mind was the movie world. Little occurred in the business that she didn't know about, either through friends or through her constant reading of the trade and fan magazines.

She knew about the arrival in Hollywood of British director Alfred Hitchcock, and she knew his already impressive roster of screen credits. With typical Lombard finesse, she pulled off a major coup by getting Hitchcock to direct her next film—which would also mark her return to comedy—*Mr. and Mrs. Smith* (1941).

Hitchcock would later tell Francois Truffaut, "That picture was done as a friendly gesture to Carole Lombard. At the time, she was married to Clark Gable, and she asked whether I'd do a picture with her. In a weak moment I accepted, and I more or less followed Norman Krasna's screenplay. Since I really didn't understand the type of people who were portrayed in the film, all I did was to photograph the scenes as written."*

As written, *Mr. and Mrs. Smith* is a silly little charade for Carole and expert farceur Robert Montgomery, with Gene Raymond as the third corner of a romantic triangle. Ann and David Smith have a perfectly happy marriage,

* Truffaut, Francois, *Hitchcock*, Simon and Schuster, New York, 1967, p. 100.

133

MR. AND MRS. SMITH (1941). With Gene Raymond

with one rather unusual ground-rule: whenever they have an argument, neither one can leave the room until the conflict is resolved. The film opens in their bedroom, where they've been together for *days*.

Real conflict arises when it's discovered that due to complicated reasons, their marriage license isn't legal, and they must be remarried. David's failure to tell Ann right away (although she's already gotten the news herself) causes her to suspect her husband's integrity and intentions, and this escalates into a separation. His love is as strong as ever, but she stubbornly spurns his advances, turning instead to his handsome law partner Jeff (Gene Raymond). The action culminates at a ski lodge where David follows Ann and Jeff, determined to win back his wife. After a prolonged comedy of errors, he does.

Mr. and Mrs. Smith is paper-thin, but it comes across as a pleasant if not superior comedy. Montgomery snatches the honors away from Carole, whose role (again) is so irrational as to tax the most charitable viewer's mind. But she's delectably beautiful and a more-than-able partner in the fun. The film's funniest scene has her and Raymond attending the New York World's Fair and getting stuck midway down the parachute jump—whereupon it rains.

When it came time to film

Hitchcock's cameo appearance, Lombard took the director's reins, and bullied "actor" Hitchcock mercilessly . . . all of which made good copy, and was even photographed for an episode of RKO's short subject series, *Picture People*.

The film didn't do much for anyone's career, but most critics agreed that it was nice to have Carole Lombard back in the world of comedy.

She remained in that world for what was to be her last picture, fulfilling a long-cherished ambition to work with director Ernst Lubitsch. Concerned with her marriage (which rumors claimed to be in shaky condition) and unwilling to make another film just to keep busy. Carole waited one year for the right picture to come alone. It was Lubitsch's *To Be or Not To Be* (1942).

Produced independently at United Artists' studio, the film was, according to biographer Larry Swindell, "the happiest experience of her career—the one time, she said, when everything began right, stayed right, and ended right."

The finished film is much the same: a brilliant topical comedy whose wisdom and humor transcend the passage of years to make it as effective in the seventies as it was in 1942. Carole is married to Jack Benny; as Maria and Joseph Tura, they are the leading lights of a popular dramatic troupe in Poland.

TO BE OR NOT TO BE (1942). With Jack Benny

TO BE OR NOT TO BE (1942). With Robert Stack

When Hitler marches into Warsaw and seizes control, their theater is darkened, but the actors perform nonetheless, in a real-life drama in which, disguised as Nazis and Nazi sympathizers, they bamboozle the uptight Gestapo and save the Polish underground movement.

Jack Benny, in an extension of his well-established comic character from radio, has the dominant starring role. But *To Be or Not To Be* is an ensemble picture, with equally memorable contributions by such players as Tom Dugan (who impersonates Hitler), Sig Ruman (as the bumptious Nazi), and Felix Bressart (as a bit actor who gets his biggest break in a "performance" for the Germans). Robert Stack has one of his best early roles as a Polish aviator with a crush on Lombard.

As for Carole, she is simply radiant, whether entertaining an overenthusiastic young admirer (Stack) in her dressing room, or leading on a susceptible Nazi agent (Stanley Ridges) who's interested in her. She plays it straight, leaving the comedy to Benny; as a result, she's warm and real, intrigued by the attentions of Stack but deeply in love with her hammy husband.

To Be or Not To Be disarmed many critics and audiences, who found it uncomfortable to laugh about the Nazi situation and the plight of Poland. But Lubitsch masterfully set up his picture to emphasize the seriousness of the *background*, and only have us laugh at the incidents taking place against that setting.

To one reviewer who accused Lubitsch of callously making fun of the Warsaw bombing, he replied, "The commentary under the shots of the devastated Warsaw speaks for itself and cannot leave any doubt in the spectator's mind what my point of view and attitude is towards these acts of horror. What I have satirized in this picture are the Nazis and their ridiculous ideology. I have also satirized the attitude of actors who always remain actors regardless of how dangerous the situation might be . . ."

To Be or Not To Be won Carole some of the best reviews of her career, including this rave from James Shelley Hamilton in the *National Board of Review Magazine*: "She shows better than ever before those rare qualities of a fine comedienne, an intelligent mind and a blithe spirit expressing themselves easily and gracefully through an assured technique of acting."

Tragically, those reviews were posthumous, for *To Be or Not To Be* was released just one month after Carole Lombard's untimely death.

TO BE OR NOT TO BE (1942). With Jack Benny and the principal players

Clark Gable was heartbroken, but he merely echoed the sentiments of many others: why did Carole Lombard have to die?

It didn't seem possible. She was life itself: vibrant, beautiful, eternally fresh and spontaneous.

Everyone in Hollywood adored her. America mourned her passing as a national tragedy.

It happened as Carole was returning from a hugely successful tour selling U.S. Defense Bonds. Accompanied by her mother and MGM press agent Otto Winkler, a friend of Gable's, they had wrapped up their junket in the capital of Carole's home state, Indiana, where in one day she sold a record two million dollars in bonds, using the charm, acting skill, and conviction she brought to every screen performance.

The Lombard party was due to return to Hollywood by train, but Carole was impatient and insisted that they fly. Her mother was nervous, and Winkler was just as happy to take the train, but Carole persisted, and they took a westbound plane that made several stops along the way. After refueling in Las Vegas the plane headed for Burbank but strayed off-course and crashed into the side of a mountain just thirty miles from Vegas. All passengers and crew died instantly. It was 7:07 P.M. on January 16, 1942.

Gable rushed to the site of the

THERE'LL NEVER BE ANOTHER

crash, and tried to reach the wreckage up the mountain, but was persuaded to turn back by official rescue teams who were having a difficult time themselves.

He returned to Hollywood a broken man.

Some have speculated that Lombard was eager to return home because she suspected her husband was seeing too much of co-star Lana Turner, with whom he was filming *Somewhere I'll Find You* . . . and that Gable's knowledge of this was the cause of his overwhelming guilt over Carole's death.

Biographer Larry Swindell has written that the Gable-Lombard marriage was not quite as idyllic as the public was led to believe, that Gable's selfishness made it necessary for the union to exist on his terms or not at all. But Carole loved him and went along with his rules.

Whatever the case, her death brought him tremendous remorse. He enlisted in the Army Air Corps and demanded the most vulnerable position in a flying team: rear gunner. It was said that without her, he hardly valued his own life.

After the war, Gable returned to movies as big a star as ever, but friends have said that in private life, he spent the rest of his years trying

One of Lombard's last glamorous photographs, taken for TO BE OR NOT TO BE

With Clark Gable at a show for Greek War Relief

to find another Carole Lombard. Moviemakers and moviegoers faced the same kind of loss. For there *was* no other Carole Lombard. She was an original.

BIBLIOGRAPHY

Basinger, Jeanine, *Shirley Temple*. Pyramid, New York, 1975.

Behlmer, Rudy (editor), *Memo from David O. Selznick,* Viking Press, New York, 1972.

Bogdanovich, Peter, *Allan Dwan: The Last Pioneer*. Praeger, New York, 1971.

Chierichetti, David, *Hollywood Director: The Career of Mitchell Leisen*. Curtis Books, New York, 1973.

Crosby, Bing (as told to Pete Martin), *Call Me Lucky*. Simon and Schuster, New York, 1953.

Deschner, Donald, *The Films of Cary Grant*. Citadel Press, Secaucus, New Jersey, 1973.

Dickens, Homer, *The Films of Gary Cooper*. Citadel Press, New York, 1970.

Essoe, Gabe, *The Films of Clark Gable*. Citadel Press, New York, 1970.

Fowler, Gene, *Good Night, Sweet Prince*. Viking Press, New York, 1944.

Harris, Warren G., *Gable and Lombard*. Simon and Schuster, New York, 1974.

Kanin, Garson, *Hollywood*. Viking Press, New York, 1974.

McBride, Joseph (editor), *Focus on Howard Hawks*. Prentice-Hall, Englewood Cliffs, New Jersey, 1972.

Milland, Ray, *Wide-Eyed in Babylon*. William Morrow, New York, 1974.

Morella, Joe and Epstein, Edward, *Gable & Lombard & Powell & Harlow*. Dell Books, New York, 1975.

Munden, Kenneth W. (Executive editor), *The American Film Institute Catalog: Feature Films 1921-30*. R. R. Bowker, New York, 1971.

Niven, David, *Bring on the Empty Horses*. G. P. Putnam's, New York, 1971.

Ott, Frederick W., *The Films of Carole Lombard*. Citadel Press, Secaucus, New Jersey, 1972.

Quinn, Anthony, *The Original Sin*. Little, Brown and Co., Boston, 1972.

Quirk, Lawrence J., *The Films of Fredric March*. Citadel Press, New York, 1971.

Rubin, Benny, *Come Backstage With Me*. Bowling Green University Popular Press, undated, Bowling Green, Ohio.

St. Johns, Adela Rogers, *The Honeycomb*. Doubleday, Garden City, New York, 1969.

Swindell, Larry, *Screwball: The Life of Carole Lombard*. William Morrow, New York, 1975.

Thomas, Bob, *Selznick*. Doubleday, Garden City, New York, 1970.
Truffaut, François, *Hitchcock*. Simon and Schuster, New York, 1967.
Turconi, David, *Mack Sennett*. Editions Seghers, Paris, 1966.
Weinberg, Herman G., *The Lubitsch Touch*. E. P. Dutton, New York, 1968.
Yablonsky, Lewis, *George Raft*. McGraw-Hill, New York, 1974.

Also:
Greenberg, Joel, "The Other Lang: an interview with Walter Lang," *Focus on Film,* Issue 18, 1974.
Uncredited and undated, "Carole Lombard's Life Story," magazine published shortly after her death.
Various issues of *Motion Picture Herald*.

THE FILMS OF CAROLE LOMBARD

The director's name follows the release date. Sp indicates screenplay and b/o indicates based/on.

1. A PERFECT CRIME. Associated, 1921. *Allan Dwan.* Sp: Allan Dwan, b/o story by Carl Clausen. Cast: Monte Blue, Jacqueline Logan, Stanton Heck, Hardee Kirkland. Silent.

2. GOLD AND THE GIRL. Fox, 1925. *Edmund Mortimer.* Sp: John Stone. Cast: Buck Jones, Elinor Fair, Bruce Gordon, Lucien Littlefield, Claude Peyton, Alphonse Ethier, Pal the Dog. Silent.

3. MARRIAGE IN TRANSIT. Fox, 1925. *Roy William Neill.* Sp: Dorothy Yost, b/o novel by Grace Lutz. Cast: Edmund Lowe, Adolph Milar, Frank Beal, Harvey Clark, Wade Boteler, Fred Walton. Silent.

4. HEARTS AND SPURS. Fox, 1925. *W. S. Van Dyke.* Sp: John Stone, b/o story by Jackson Gregory. Cast: Buck Jones, William Davidson, Freeman Wood, Jean Lamott. Silent.

5. DURAND OF THE BADLANDS. Fox, 1925. *Lynn Reynolds.* Sp: Lynn Reynolds, b/o story by Maibelle Justice. Cast: Buck Jones, Marion Nixon, Malcolm Waite, Fred De Silva, Luke Cosgrove. Silent.

6. THE ROAD TO GLORY. Fox, 1926. *Howard Hawks.* Sp: L. G. Rigby, b/o story by Howard Hawks. Cast: May McAvoy, Leslie Fenton, Ford Sterling, Rockliffe Fellowes, Milla Davenport, John MacSweeney. Silent.

7. SMITH'S PONY. Sennett–Pathé, 1927. *Alf Goulding.* Cast: Raymond McKee, Ruth Hiatt, Mary Ann Jackson, Billy Gilbert. Silent short-subject.

8. A GOLD DIGGER OF WEEPAH. Sennett–Pathé, 1927. *Harry Edwards.* Cast: Billy Bevan, Madeline Hurlock, Vernon Dent. Silent short-subject.

9. THE GIRL FROM EVERYWHERE. Sennett–Pathé, 1927. *Edward Cline.* Sp: Harry McCoy and Vernon Smith. Cast: Daphne Pollard, Dot Farley, Mack Swain, Irving Bacon, Madalynne Fields. Silent short-subject.

10.   RUN, GIRL, RUN. Sennett–Pathé, 1928. *Alf Goulding.* Sp: Harry McCoy and James Tynan. Cast: Daphne Pollard, Irving Bacon, Dot Farley, Madalynne Fields. Silent short-subject, in color.

11.   THE BEACH CLUB. Sennett–Pathé, 1928. *Harry Edwards.* Sp: Jefferson Moffitt and Harry McCoy. Cast: Billy Bevan, Madeline Hurlock, Vernon Dent. Silent short-subject.

12.   THE BEST MAN. Sennett–Pathé, 1928. *Harry Edwards.* Cast: Billy Bevan, Alma Bennett, Vernon Dent, Andy Clyde, Billy Searby. Silent short-subject.

13.   THE SWIM PRINCESS. Sennett–Pathé, 1928. *Alf Goulding.* Sp: James Tynan and Frank Capra. Cast: Daphne Pollard, Andy Clyde, Cissie Fitzgerald. Silent short-subject, in color.

14.   THE BICYCLE FLIRT. Sennett–Pathé, 1928. *Harry Edwards.* Sp: Vernon Smith and Harry McCoy. Cast: Billy Bevan, Vernon Dent, Dot Farley. Silent short-subject.

15.   THE DIVINE SINNER. Rayart, 1928. *Scott Pembroke.* Sp: Robert Anthony Dillon. Cast: Vera Reynolds, Nigel De Brulier, Bernard Seigel, Ernest Hilliard. Silent.

16.   THE GIRL FROM NOWHERE. Sennett–Pathé, 1928. *Harry Edwards.* Sp: Ewart Anderson and Jefferson Moffitt. Cast: Daphne Pollard, Dot Farley, Mack Swain, Sterling Holloway, Madalynne Fields. Silent short-subject.

17.   HIS UNLUCKY NIGHT. Sennett–Pathé, 1928. *Harry Edwards.* Sp: Vernon Smith and Nick Barrows. Cast: Billy Bevan, Vernon Dent, Dot Farley, Bud Jamison, Andy Clyde. Silent short-subject.

18.   THE CAMPUS CARMEN. Sennett–Pathé, 1928. *Alf Goulding.* Sp: Jefferson Moffitt and Earle Rodney. Cast: Daphne Pollard, Madalynne Fields, Johnny Burke. Silent short-subject, in color.

19.   POWER. Pathe, 1928. *Howard Higgin.* Sp: Tay Garnett. Titles: John Kraft. Cast: William Boyd, Alan Hale, Jacqueline Logan, Jerry Drew, Joan Bennett, Pauline Curley. Silent.

20.   ME, GANGSTER. Fox, 1928. *Raoul Walsh.* Sp: Charles Francis Coe and Raoul Walsh, b/o story by Charles Francis Coe. Cast: June Collyer, Don Terry, Anders Randolf, Stella Adams, Al Hill, Burr McIntosh, Walter James, Gustav von Seyffertitz. Silent.

21. SHOW FOLKS. Pathe, 1928. *Paul L. Stein.* Sp: Jack Jungmeyer and George Dromgold, b/o story by Phillip Dunning. Titles: John Kraft. Cast: Eddie Quillan, Lina Basquette, Robert Armstrong, Crauford Kent, Bessie Barriscale, Maurice Black. Silent; talking sequence.

22. THE CAMPUS VAMP. Sennett–Pathé, 1928. *Harry Edwards.* Cast: Sally Eilers, Matty Kemp, Madalynne Fields, Vernon Dent, Carmelita Geraghty. Silent short-subject.

23. NED McCOBB'S DAUGHTER. Pathé, 1928. *William J. Cowen.* Sp: Marie Beulah Dix, b/o play by Sidney Howard. Titles: John Kraft. Cast: Irene Rich, Theodore Roberts, Robert Armstrong, George Baeraud, George Hearn, Louis Natheaux. Silent; synchronized soundtrack.

24. MATCHMAKING MAMAS. Sennett–Pathé, 1929. *Harry Edwards.* Sp: Jefferson Moffitt and Carl Harbaugh. Cast: Johnny Burke, Sally Eilers, Matty Kemp. Silent short-subject.

25. HIGH VOLTAGE. Pathe, 1929. *Howard Higgin.* Sp: Elliott Clawson, James Gleason. Cast: William Boyd, Diane Ellis, Owen Moore, Billy Bevan, Phillips Smalley, Lee Shumway.

26. BIG NEWS. Pathe, 1929. *Gregory La Cava.* Sp: Walter DeLeon, Jack Jungmeyer, Frank Reicher, b/o play by George S. Brooks. Cast: Robert Armstrong, Tom Kennedy, Sam Hardy, Louis Payne, Wade Boteler, Charles Sellon.

27. THE RACKETEER. Pathé, 1930. *Howard Higgin.* Sp: Paul Gangelin and A. A. Kline. Cast: Robert Armstrong, Roland Drew, Paul Hurst, Hedda Hopper, Jeanette Loff, John Loder, Winter Hall, Winifred Harris.

28. THE ARIZONA KID. Fox, 1930. *Alfred Santell.* Sp: Ralph Block and Joseph Wright, b/o story by Ralph Block. Cast: Warner Baxter, Mona Maris, Theodore von Eltz, Mrs. Jimenez, Arthur Stone, Walter P. Lewis, Jack Herrick, Wilfred Lucas, Hank Mann, De Sacia Mooers.

29. SAFETY IN NUMBERS. Paramount, 1930. *Victor Schertzinger.* Sp: Marion Dix, b/o story by George Marion, Jr., and Percy Heath. Cast: Charles "Buddy" Rogers, Kathryn Crawford, Josephine Dunn, Geneva Mitchell, Roscoe Karns, Francis McDonald, Virginia Bruce, Richard Tucker, Raoul Paoli, Lawrence Grant, Louise Beavers.

30. FAST AND LOOSE. Paramount, 1930. *Fred Newmeyer.* Sp: Doris Anderson and Preston Sturges, b/o David Gray's adaptation of play by Avery Hopwood. Cast: Miriam Hopkins, Frank Morgan, Charles Starrett, Henry Wadsworth, Winifred Harris, Herbert Yost, David Hutcheson, Ilka Chase. Previously filmed in 1925.

31. IT PAYS TO ADVERTISE. Paramount, 1931. *Frank Tuttle.* Sp: Arthur Kober, b/o play by Rol Cooper Megrue and Walter Hackett. Cast: Norman Foster, Skeets Gallagher, Eugene Pallette, Lucien Littlefield, Helen Johnson, Louise Brooks, Morgan Wallace, Marcia Manners, Tom Kennedy. Previously filmed in 1919.

32. MAN OF THE WORLD. Paramount, 1931. *Richard Wallace.* Sp: Herman J. Mankiewicz. Cast: William Powell, Wynne Gibson, Guy Kibbee, Lawrence Gray, Tom Ricketts, Andre Cheron, George Chandler, Tom Costello, Maude Truax.

33. LADIES' MAN. Paramount, 1931. *Lothar Mendes.* Sp: Herman J. Mankiewicz, b/o story by Rupert Hughes. Cast: William Powell, Kay Francis, Gilbert Emery, Olive Tell, Martin Burton, John Holland, Frank Atkinson, Maude Turner Gordon.

34. UP POPS THE DEVIL. Paramount, 1931. *Edward Sutherland.* Sp: Arthur Kober and Eve Unsell, b/o play by Albert Hackett and Frances Goodrich. Cast: Norman Foster, Skeets Gallagher, Stuart Erwin, Lilyan Tashman, Edward J. Nugent, Theodore von Eltz, Joyce Compton, Sleep 'n' Eat (Willie Best). Remade in 1938 as *Thanks For the Memory.*

35. I TAKE THIS WOMAN. Paramount, 1931. *Marion Gering and Slavko Vorkapich.* Sp: Vincent Lawrence, b/o novel by Mary Roberts Rinehart. Cast: Gary Cooper, Helen Ware, Lester Vail, Charles Trowbridge, Clara Blandick.

36. NO ONE MAN. Paramount, 1932. *Lloyd Corrigan.* Sp: Sidney Buchman, Agnes Brand Leahy, and Percy Heath, b/o novel by Rupert Hughes. Cast: Ricardo Cortez, Paul Lukas, Juliette Compton, George Barbier, Virginia Hammond, Arthur Pierson, Francis Moffett, Irving Bacon.

37. SINNERS IN THE SUN. Paramount, 1932. *Alexander Hall.* Sp: Vincent Lawrence, Waldemar Young, and Samuel Hoffenstein, b/o story by Mildred Cram. Cast: Chester Morris, Adrienne Ames, Alison Skipworth, Walter Byron, Reginald Barlow, Zita Moulton, Cary Grant, Luke Cosgrove, Ida Lewis.

38. VIRTUE. Columbia, 1932. *Edward Buzzell.* Sp: Robert Riskin, b/o story by Ethel Hill. Cast: Pat O'Brien, Ward Bond, Willard Robertson, Shirley Grey, Ed Le Saint, Jack LaRue, Mayo Methot.

39. NO MORE ORCHIDS. Columbia, 1932. *Walter Lang.* Sp: Gertrude Purcell, b/o story by Grace Perkins, adapted by Keene Thompson. Cast: Walter Connolly, Louise Closser Hale, Lyle Talbot, Allen Vincent, Ruthelma Stevens, C. Aubrey Smith, William V. Mong.

40. NO MAN OF HER OWN. Paramount, 1932. *Wesley Ruggles*. Sp: Maurine Watkins and Milton Gropper, b/o story by Edmund Goulding and Benjamin Glazer. Cast: Clark Gable. Dorothy Mackaill, Grant Mitchell, George Barbier, Elizabeth Patterson, J. Farrell Macdonald, Tommy Conlon.

41. FROM HELL TO HEAVEN. Paramount, 1933. *Erle C. Kenton*. Sp: Percy Heath and Sidney Buchman, b/o play by Lawrence Hazard. Cast: Jack Oakie, Adrienne Ames, David Manners, Sidney Blackmer, Verna Hillie, James C. Eagles, Shirley Grey, Bradley Page, Walter Walker, Berton Churchill, Donald Kerr, Nydia Westman, Cecil Cunningham.

42. SUPERNATURAL. Paramount, 1933. *Victor Halperin*. Sp: Harvey Thew and Brian Marlow, b/o story by Garnett Weston. Cast: Randolph Scott, Vivienne Osborne, Alan Dinehart, H. B. Warner, Beryl Mercer, William Farnum.

43. THE EAGLE AND THE HAWK. Paramount, 1933. *Mitchell Leisen and Stuart Walker*. Sp: Bogart Rogers and Seton I. Miller, b/o story by John Monk Saunders. Cast: Fredric March, Cary Grant, Jack Oakie, Sir Guy Standing, Forrester Harvey, Kenneth Howell, Leland Hodgson, Virginia Hammond, Crauford Kent, Douglas Scott, Robert Manning.

44. BRIEF MOMENT. Columbia, 1933. *David Burton*. Sp: Brian Marlow and Edith Fitzgerald, b/o play by S. N. Behrman. Cast: Gene Raymond, Monroe Owsley, Donald Cook, Arthur Hohl, Reginald Mason, Jameson Thomas, Theresa Maxwell Conover.

45. WHITE WOMAN. Paramount, 1933. *Stuart Walker*. Sp: Samuel Hoffenstein and Gladys Lehman, b/o story by Norman Reilly Raine and Frank Butler. Cast: Charles Laughton, Charles Bickford, Kent Taylor, Percy Kilbride, Charles Middleton, James Bell, Claude King, Ethel Griffies, Jimmie Dime, Marc Lawrence, Mabel Johnson.

46. BOLERO. Paramount, 1934. *Wesley Ruggles*. Sp: Horace Jackson, b/o story by Carey Wilson and Kubec Glasmon, from idea by Ruth Ridenour. Cast: George Raft, William Frawley, Frances Drake, Sally Rand, Ray Milland, Gloria Shea, Gertrude Michael, Del Henderson, Frank G. Dunn.

47. WE'RE NOT DRESSING. Paramount, 1934. *Norman Taurog*. Sp: Horace Jackson, Francis Martin, and George Marion, Jr., b/o story by Benjamin Glazer from novel by Sir James Barrie. Cast: Bing Crosby, George Burns, Gracie Allen, Ethel Merman, Leon Errol, Jay Henry, Ray Milland, John Irwin, Charles Morris, Ben Hendricks, Ted Oliver.

48. 20TH CENTURY. Columbia, 1934. *Howard Hawks.* Sp. Ben Hecht and Charles MacArthur, b/o their play. Cast: John Barrymore, Walter Connolly, Roscoe Karns, Charles Levison (Lane), Etienne Girardot, Dale Fuller, Ralph Forbes, Edgar Kennedy, Ed Gargan.

49. NOW AND FOREVER. Paramount, 1934. *Henry Hathaway.* Sp: Vincent Lawrence and Sylvia Thalliery, b/o story by Jack Kirkland and Melville Baker. Cast: Gary Cooper, Shirley Temple, Sir Guy Standing, Charlotte Granville, Gilbert Emery, Henry Kolker, Tetsu Komai, Jameson Thomas, Harry Stubbe, Egon Brecher.

50. LADY BY CHOICE. Columbia, 1934. *David Burton.* Sp: Jo Swerling, b/o story by Dwight Taylor. Cast: May Robson, Roger Pryor, Walter Connolly, Arthur Hohl, Raymond Walburn, James Burke, Mariska Aldrich, John Doyle, Henry Kolker, Lillian Harmer, Abe Denovitch.

51. THE GAY BRIDE. MGM, 1934. *Jack Conway.* Sp: Samuel and Bella Spewack, b/o story by Charles Francis Coe. Cast: Chester Morris, ZaSu Pitts, Leo Carrillo, Nat Pendleton, Sam Hardy, Walter Walker.

52. RUMBA. Paramount, 1935. *Marion Gering.* Sp: Howard J. Green, Harry Ruskin, Frank Partas, b/o story by Guy Endore and Seena Owen. Cast: George Raft, Lynne Overman, Margo, Monroe Owsley, Iris Adrian, Samuel S. Hinds, Virginia Hammond, Gail Patrick, Akim Tamiroff.

53. HANDS ACROSS THE TABLE. Paramount, 1935. *Mitchell Leisen.* Sp: Norman Krasna, Vincent Lawrence, and Herbert Fields, b/o story by Vina Delmar. Cast: Fred MacMurray, Ralph Bellamy, Astrid Allwyn, Ruth Donnelly, Marie Prevost, Joseph Tozer, William Demarest, Ed Gargan, Ferdinand Munier, Harold Minjir, Marcelle Corday.

54. LOVE BEFORE BREAKFAST. Universal, 1936. *Walter Lang.* Sp: Herbert Fields, b/o novel by Faith Baldwin. Cast: Preston Foster, Janet Beecher, Cesar Romero, Betty Lawford, Douglas Blackley, Don Briggs, Bert Roach, Andre Beranger, Richard Carle, Ed Barton.

55. THE PRINCESS COMES ACROSS. Paramount, 1936. *William K. Howard.* Sp: Walter De Leon, Francis Martin, Frank Butler, and Don Hartman, b/o story by Philip MacDonald, from novel by Louis Lucien Rogger. Cast: Fred MacMurray, Douglass Dumbrille, Alison Skipworth, William Frawley, Porter Hall, George Barbier, Lumsden Hare, Sig Ruman, Mischa Auer, Tetsu Komai, Bradley Page, Bennie Bartlett.

56. MY MAN GODFREY. Universal, 1936. *Gregory La Cava.* Sp: Morrie Ryskind and Eric Hatch, b/o novel by Eric Hatch. Cast: William Powell, Alice Brady, Gail Patrick, Jean Dixon, Eugene Pallette, Alan Mowbray, Mischa Auer, Robert Light, Pat Flaherty, Franklin Pangborn, Grady Sutton. Remade in 1957.

57. SWING HIGH, SWING LOW. Paramount, 1937. *Mitchell Leisen.* Sp: Virginia Van Upp and Oscar Hammerstein II, b/o play by George Manker Watters and Arthur Hopkins. Cast: Fred MacMurray, Charles Butterworth, Jean Dixon, Dorothy Lamour, Harvey Stephens, Cecil Cunningham, Charlie Arnt, Franklin Pangborn, Anthony Quinn. Previously filmed in 1929 as *The Dance of Life* and remade in 1948 as *When My Baby Smiles at Me.*

58. NOTHING SACRED. Selznick/United Artists, 1937. *William Wellman.* Sp: Ben Hecht, b/o story by William Street. Cast: Fredric March, Charles Winninger, Walter Connolly, Sig Ruman, Frank Fay, Raymond Scott Quintet, Maxie Rosenbloom, Alex Schoenberg, Monty Woolley, Margaret Hamilton. In color. Remade in 1954 as *Living It Up.*

59. TRUE CONFESSION. Paramount, 1937. *Wesley Ruggles.* Sp: Claude Binyon, b/o play by Louis Verneuil and Georges Berr. Cast: Fred MacMurray, John Barrymore, Una Merkel, Porter Hall, Edgar Kennedy, Lynn Overman, Fritz Feld, Richard Carle, John T. Murray. Remade in 1946 as *Cross My Heart.*

60. FOOLS FOR SCANDAL. Warner Bros., 1938. *Mervyn Le Roy.* Sp: Herbert Fields, Joseph Fields, and Irving Brecher, b/o play by Nancy Hamilton, James Shute, and Rosemary Casey. Cast: Fernand Gravet, Ralph Bellamy, Allen Jenkins, Isabel Jeans, Marie Wilson, Marcia Ralston, Tola Nesmith, Heather Thatcher, Jacques Lory.

61. MADE FOR EACH OTHER. Selznick/United Artists, 1939. *John Cromwell.* Sp: Jo Swerling. Cast: James Stewart, Charles Coburn, Lucile Watson, Eddie Quillan, Alma Kruger, Ruth Weston, Donald Briggs, Harry Davenport, Esther Dale, Renee Orsell, Louise Beavers, Ward Bond.

62. IN NAME ONLY. RKO, 1939. *John Cromwell.* Sp: Richard Sherman, b/o novel by Bessie Breuer. Cast: Cary Grant, Kay Francis, Charles Coburn, Helen Vinson, Katharine Alexander, Jonathan Hale, Maurice Moscovich, Nella Walker, Peggy Ann Garner, Spencer Charters.

63. VIGIL IN THE NIGHT. RKO, 1940. *George Stevens.* Sp: Fred Guiol, P. J. Wolfson, Rowland Leigh, b/o novel by A. J. Cronin. Cast: Brian Aherne, Anne Shirley, Julien Mitchell, Robert Coote, Brenda Forbes, Rita Page, Peter Cushing, Ethel Griffies, Doris Lloyd, Emily Fitzroy.

64.   THEY KNEW WHAT THEY WANTED. RKO, 1940. *Garson Kanin*. Sp: Robert Ardrey, b/o play by Sidney Howard. Cast: Charles Laughton, William Gargan, Harry Carey, Frank Fay, Joe Bernard, Janet Fox, Lee Tung-Foo, Karl Malden, Victor Kilian, Paul Lepers, Tom Ewell. Previously filmed in 1928 as *The Secret Hour* and in 1930 as *A Lady to Love*.

65.   MR. AND MRS. SMITH. RKO, 1941. *Alfred Hitchcock*. Sp: Norman Krasna. Cast: Robert Montgomery, Gene Raymond, Jack Carson, Philip Merivale, Lucile Watson, William Tracy, Charles Halton, Esther Dale, Emma Dunn, William Edmunds, Betty Compson.

66.   TO BE OR NOT TO BE. United Artists, 1942. *Ernst Lubitsch*. Sp: Edwin Justis Mayer, b/o story by Ernst Lubitsch and Melchior Lengyel. Cast: Jack Benny, Robert Stack, Felix Bressart, Lionel Atwill, Stanley Ridges, Sig Ruman, Tom Dugan, Charles Halton, Henry Victor, Maude Eburne.

Lombard also appeared in RKO's short subject PICTURE PEOPLE #4 (1940), and reportedly can be seen in DICK TURPIN (Fox, 1925), HALF A BRIDE (Paramount, 1928), and DYNAMITE (MGM, 1929) from which films she was officially cut. There is also a possibility that she appeared in THE FIGHTING EAGLE (Pathé, 1927) but this is based on circumstantial evidence.

INDEX

153

ABOUT THE AUTHOR

Leonard Maltin has written many books on film, including *TV Movies, Movie Comedy Teams, Behind the Camera, The Great Movie Shorts,* and *The Disney Films.* He is also General Editor of the Popular Library Film Series, and for nine years edited and published *Film Fan Monthly* magazine. His articles have appeared in *The New York Times, Esquire, TV Guide, Saturday Review,* and other publications. He teaches at the New School for Social Research in New York, and lectures on film around the country.

ABOUT THE EDITOR

Ted Sennett is the author of *Warner Brothers Presents,* a tribute to the great Warners films of the thirties and forties, and of *Lunatics and Lovers,* on the long-vanished but well-remembered "screwball" movie comedies of the past. He is also the editor of *The Movie Buff's Book* and has written about films for magazines and newspapers. He lives in New Jersey with his wife and three children.